An Independent Woman

KATHARINE
HEPBURN

An Independent Woman

KATHARINE HEPBURN

RONALD BERGAN

BLOOMSBURY

First published in Great Britain 1996
Bloomsbury Publishing Plc
2 Soho Square
London W1V 6HB

A CIP catalogue record for this book is
available from the British Library

ISBN 0 7475 2215 4

10 9 8 7 6 5 4 3 2 1

Designed by Bradbury and Williams
Picture research by Juliet Brightmore
Printed in Hong Kong

Contents

Author's Note and Acknowledgements

Katharine Hepburn was eighty-seven years old when I visited her at her house on East 49th Street in New York in the spring of 1995. A few months previously, a biography of Katharine Hepburn by Barbara Leaming had been published. Although Kate herself refused to go into print on the subject, in private she was outraged and upset by the book's 'inaccuracies', and what she saw as a betrayal of her confidences. A number of people with special and personal knowledge, including Kate's niece Katharine Houghton, John Ford's grandson, and Selden West, the authorized biographer of Spencer Tracy, attacked the book's 'distortions'. Their main complaints were that Leaming had painted an erroneously negative picture of Tracy and his attitude towards Kate, and exaggerated the importance of Ford's relationship with the star, building a false psychological structure upon it.

It is not my intention to condemn the work of a fellow biographer, only to explain the book's effect on Kate and her family and friends when I approached her to comment on the pictures contained within these pages. In the light of the appearance of the Leaming book, Kate was naturally wary about talking to any other writer, and was reluctant to be drawn on this plainly disagreeable matter. Nevertheless, she was willing to allow me into her home, where she signed my copy of her autobiography, *Me*, and made a number of perceptive and penetrating remarks about her career, which I have included in this celebration of her life and work.

I have tried, as much as possible, to avoid speculation, and to weed out the myths that inevitably grow around a Hollywood legend. To this purpose, I have put my trust in much of what Kate has said in interviews and written about herself, and in those who knew her well, as well as in Anne Edwards' excellent biography (Hodder and Stoughton, 1985). But I was merely responsible for the text, and had only a small hand in the selection of the illustrative material in a book which, I feel, is eloquent proof of the adage that pictures speak louder than words.

I have cause to be grateful to the following people (in alphabetical order): Zelda Baron for choice anecdotes; Juliet Brightmore for her taste and eye for a good photograph; Howard and Ron Mandelbaum at Photofest, who anticipated my every need; Penny Phillips, who had the perspicacity to commission the book and supported me throughout; and Sharon Powers, Katharine Hepburn's congenial and most helpful secretary, who went out of her way to pave a way for my visit to Kate's home. Most of all, I am grateful to Katharine Hepburn, for her grace, intelligence, enduring beauty and radiant smile.

RONALD BERGAN, LONDON 1996

FOR LESLIE, WHEREVER YOU MAY BE.

Introduction

I'm a personality as well as an actress.
Show me an actress who isn't a
personality, and you'll show me a
woman who isn't a star.

'A handsome woman of great temperament, authority, and presence. She has been a queen of international importance for forty-six years and you know it. Finally, she is that most unusual thing: a genuine feminine woman thoroughly capable of holding her own in a man's world.' This was how James Goldman pictured the character of Eleanor of Aquitaine in his play *The Lion in Winter*, an apt description of Katharine Hepburn herself at the peak of her profession. But it was not an easy or a straightforward climb to the top.

Given her nature, it is understandable that Katharine Hepburn, more than any other screen actress, has irritated as many people as she has enraptured. Among the great female movie stars, she is perhaps the most difficult to categorize. With her singular looks, the distinctive cadences of her voice and her complete disregard for the conventions of conservative Hollywood, she followed her own path, in films – where her choice of roles often reflected her own personality and beliefs – and in life.

As an actress, she was both robust and vulnerable, tough-minded yet sentimental, delivering lines in a voice that Hepburn herself described as 'a cross between Donald Duck and a Stradivarius'. She was a curious mixture of liberated and submissive woman, platonic and sexual beauty, scrawny spinster, waif and androgyne. Although she played the rebel daughter in many of her early successes, the Hepburn image seems always to have been of a slightly shocking, eccentric aunt. What she demonstrated, above all, on screen and off, were the pleasures, pains and possibilities of independence.

Katharine Hepburn at the beginning of her screen career in the early 1930s, when Hollywood was unsure how to present this singular personality to the public.

However, most of the men she fell for dominated her to a large extent, and she remained closely tied to her parents, heavily dependent on their approval. 'I'm like the girl who never grew up,' she once said. 'I just never really left home, so to speak. I always went back there almost every weekend of my life when I wasn't filming. I kept my life there... my roots.'

When Hepburn arrived in Hollywood in 1932, RKO studio executives described her as looking 'like a cross between a horse and a monkey', and George Cukor characterized her as 'a boa-constrictor on a fast'. She wasn't a long-stemmed American beauty, a seductive foreign vamp, a cute, golden-haired 'sweetheart', or a defenceless tragic heroine; she was decidedly a modern, emancipated woman, with a purposeful stride.

In a memo to his staff, David Selznick, rejecting her for the role of Scarlett O'Hara in his production of *Gone with the Wind*, wrote, 'Hepburn has two strikes against her – first, the unquestionable and very widespread intense public dislike of her at this moment, and second, the fact that she has yet to demonstrate the sex qualities that are probably the most important of all the many requisites of Scarlett.'

But she had confounded everyone, helped somewhat by Hollywood's glamour treatment, by emerging, with her high cheekbones and natural looks, as a stunning beauty. Her beauty grew out of her own belief in herself, exposing her own nerves and vulnerability, along with her intelligence and sensibility.

From her first appearance on the screen as John Barrymore's daughter in *A Bill of Divorcement* (1932), Hepburn was a breath of fresh air. She won her first Oscar in her third screen role in *Morning Glory* (1932), playing Eva Lovelace, a young actress who comes to New York determined to succeed on the stage and prove she is 'the finest actress in the world'. In her four films with Cary Grant – *Sylvia Scarlett*, *Holiday*, *Bringing Up Baby*, *The Philadelphia Story* – she was radiant, full of spirit and sexuality which he brought out in her, offering that rare combination of wit and emotional intensity.

Yet, for years, especially outside the big cities, she remained a minority or acquired taste, rarely appealing to Southern or Midwestern audiences. People couldn't relate to her. She wasn't selling sex or wholesomeness or glamour, the commodities most leading ladies dealt in, and her originality wasn't the sort that shopgirls could identify with or men fantasize about. She always appeared irreverent and very self-assured, threatening or challenging male supremacy. Children laughed at her diction and aristocratic airs. She had been dubbed 'Katharine of Arrogance'. Hepburn's fans came from the middle-aged, sophisticated portion of film audiences, but even this group was frequently put off by the fluttery mannerisms and pretensions of her worst films. Inevitably, in the 1930s, she gained the label of 'box-office poison'.

Richard Watts in the *Herald Tribune* spoke for many people when he began his review of *The Philadelphia Story* with a tribute to Hepburn's pluck. 'Few actresses have been so relentlessly assailed by critics, wits, columnists, magazine editors, and other professional assailers over so long a period of time, and even if you confess that some of the abuse had a certain amount of justification to it, you must admit she faced it gamely and unflinchingly and fought back with courage and gallantry.'

Katharine Hepburn's career straddled seven decades, proving that 'age cannot wither her, nor custom stale her infinite variety'. There are performers whose physique tends to type-cast them in historical roles, others who cannot appear anything but contemporary. Kate's style might be described as timeless. Thus there was no incongruity in her winning an Oscar for her suburban wife and mother in *Guess Who's Coming to Dinner?* as well as for her witty, patrician, strong-willed Queen Eleanor of Aquitaine, the estranged wife of King Henry II in *The Lion in Winter* in successive years. With *On Golden Pond*, she became the first performer to win four Best Actress Oscars, from a record twelve nominations, an achievement as yet unsurpassed.

As she matured, she was admired for the very reasons she had once been despised. Just as in life she had initially alienated many people by her haughty and assertive manner, and then won them over completely, so Katharine Hepburn finally conquered the movie-going public. She became a member of the select group of Hollywood favourites who are mythic embodiments of certain values such as independence and integrity, cherished by American audiences. How Katharine Hepburn moved from the awkward, flamboyant, tempestuous, self-opinionated girl and 'box-office poison' to become, in her own phrase, 'Saint Katharine', I hope the following pages will make clear.

Kate in 1975, after four decades in films, relaxing in her habitual casual clothes and manner at her New York home, surrounded by books and flowers.

1

Redtop

*Mother and Dad were perfect parents.
They brought us up with a feeling of
freedom. There were no rules. There were
simply certain things which we did —
and certain things which we didn't do
because they would hurt others.*

Katharine Hepburn was blessed with two exceptional parents, and she knew it. She would model herself on her mother and fall for men who reminded her of her father. Perhaps she yearned in vain for her relationships with men to replicate that of her parents. Their influence on her life and work was immeasurable, and to gain any understanding of the star, it is necessary to quantify that influence.

A description of Katharine Martha Houghton, known as Kit, fits her famous daughter to a tee. A

tall, strikingly beautiful woman, headstrong, haughty and fiercely independently minded, she loved discussing politics and taboo subjects, and believed fervently in women's rights. Kit Houghton was born in Buffalo on 2 February 1878 into a rich and socially prominent family, whose money was made from a glass works. She and her two younger sisters were orphaned as children, but were assured an income and the guardianship of a wealthy uncle, Amory Bigelow Houghton, which meant moving from Buffalo to Boston. In adolescence, Kit's nonconformist ideas shocked her conservative uncle, who often threatened to cut off her allowance. But Kit insisted she and her sisters fulfil her mother's dying wish for her daughters to 'Go to college! Get an education!' Thus, Katharine Houghton went to Bryn Mawr College, situated in a suburb of Philadelphia, the first women's college to offer a Ph.D. However, by the time her own daughter went there in the 1920s, the college had acquired a snobbish reputation, renowned for rearing young ladies who spoke like her, broad 'a's, swallowed 'r's, and a rising intonation at the end of sentences. Kate would be dogged throughout her career by critics drawing attention to her Bryn Mawr accent, especially when she attempted to play characters who lay beneath the upper crust.

Kate's father, Thomas Norval Hepburn, was born on 18 December

Dr Thomas Norval Hepburn, Kate's father, aged twenty-four, in a photo taken at his graduation from the medical college of Johns Hopkins University.

Opposite: *Loving siblings. Kate (right), aged two and a half, with five-year-old brother Tom, posing on their favourite sled.*

Left: *Kate's magnificent mother and role model, Katharine Martha Houghton, in all her crusading glory, speechifying on women's rights.*

Two freckled-faced kids – shy four-year-old Kate (left) with older brother Tom, whose tragic early death was to leave a deep scar.

1879 in Hanover County, Virginia. Of Scottish descent, the Hepburns could trace their ancestry back to James Hepburn, Earl of Bothwell, third husband of Mary, Queen of Scots. This was one of the reasons that Kate wished to play the doomed queen on screen many years later, despite her antipathy towards the character.

Tom Hepburn, an athletic, handsome red-head, was a graduate student at Johns Hopkins Medical School in Baltimore when he met Kit Houghton. Just after having been introduced to him, she told her sister Edith, 'That's the one!' When Edith pointed out that the man didn't have a penny, Kit replied, 'I'd marry him even if I knew it meant I'd die in a year – and go to hell!'

In 1904, after Kit had earned a master's degree in art at Radcliffe and Tom was an intern at Hartford Hospital, they were married. Within a year, they had their first child, Thomas Houghton Hepburn. When their second child, Katharine Houghton Hepburn, was born on 12 May 1907, at 22 Hudson Street, Hartford, Connecticut, Kit, who had hoped for a red-haired child, asked the nurse to hold the baby up to the window so she could see, and then exclaimed, 'Yes, it's red!' Her family called her 'Redtop', as well as 'Kat', 'Kate' or 'Kathy'.

Though Dr and Mrs Hepburn were not considered rich by Hartford's standards, they bought their own home – an early Victorian house on Hawthorn Street – had servants and were one of the first families in the new neighbourhood to possess a car. Shaded by one of the eight giant cedars growing on the property, small Kate played by the brook that ran through her parents' land, and climbed trees.

One morning, her father opened the door to a policeman. 'Sir,' the officer reported, 'your little girl is in the top of that tallest cedar. I can see her red hair sticking out above the green.'

'For heaven's sake don't call to her,' Dr Hepburn retorted. 'You might make her fall.' He then shut the door and returned to his reading.

Shortly after Kate's birth, her mother attended a suffrage lecture given by Emmeline Pankhurst. In fact, Dr Hepburn encouraged her to go. He had read Shaw and Ibsen, who revealed to him the frustrations of the modern woman, and he knew that his wife, being a rebel at heart and dedicated to her own emancipation, would soon find the role of wife and mother too restrictive. Kate later interpreted her mother's thoughts as, 'Now this is great, and these two little things are fine, but is this the end of my contribution to the world?'

Mrs Hepburn was much impressed by the diminutive Mrs Pankhurst (they were later to become good friends), and she immediately decided to join the suffragist movement. It wasn't long before she was addressing meetings, marching and carrying banners demanding equality for women.

From the age of four, Kate was taken along to meetings and lectures with her mother. Seated either on the platform or in the front row, the child listened to her mother's booming voice as she rallied audiences to her cause. This impressed Kate no end, and throughout her life she was given to making speeches, not from a soap box, but in drawing rooms.

She would also devote a great deal of time, in her later years, to Planned Parenthood. Ironically, in the midst of her mother's campaigns for the practice of birth control, a further four Hepburn children were born: Richard (1911), Bob (1913), Marion (1918) and Peg (1920).

Dr and Mrs Hepburn taught their children that everything in life must be earned by their own efforts; nothing must be freely given or received. The children were never asked to leave the room no matter what the subject of the conversation. They sat in the parlour and listened to men and women of radical ideas discussing venereal disease, prostitution and the use of contraceptives. When Kate asked her mother, now President of the Connecticut Women's Suffrage Association, about her own birth, Mrs Hepburn explained to her 'scientifically and specifically'.

'Oh, then I can have a baby without getting married,' Kate replied. 'That's what I shall do.'

According to the author Nina Wilcox Putnam, an occasional visitor to the Hepburn household, the child was 'totally undisciplined by her clever mother'. 'I saw her take food from the plates of distinguished guests – at will and unreproved... I remember her interrupting the conversation of her elders – unreproved. I remember her snatching ladies' hats and putting them on her own head – unreproved.'

What bothered Kate most was her overabundance of freckles – they covered her from head to toe. Worried that because of them no one would want her, she confided her fears to her father.

'I want to tell you something, Kate, and you must never forget it,' he said. 'Jesus Christ, Alexander the Great and Leonardo da Vinci all had red hair and freckles, and they did all right.'

Yet, when she went to her first dance with her older brother Tom, she felt awkward, and overheard a boy ask Tom, 'Who's that goofy-looking wallflower standing over there?' An experience that,

unconsciously, must have stood her in good stead when she took on roles of a number of wallflowers, such as Alice Adams, from a young age.

At school Kate made few friends, depending mainly on Tom and her father for companionship. Every day their father led them in callisthenics, taught them wrestling holds and had them join his male friends in team matches of touch football, for which Kate had her hair cut so that the boys couldn't grab it. Winning was important to Kate, for it brought the highest praise from her father, who treated her on a par with the boys.

Dr Hepburn believed in cold baths, the colder the better, and all the children had to get used to them. 'That gave me the impression that the bitterer the medicine, the better it was for you,' Kate later commented. Cold showers were something she continued to practise into her old age.

Despite her mother's work for women's equality, and her independent nature, the Hepburn household was a classic patriarchy – though Mrs Hepburn did throw things at her husband when they argued about politics. Kate's description of her father defined her own ideal man. 'There are men of action and men of thought, and if you ever get a combination of the two – well – that's the top – you've got someone like Dad.'

Besides all sports, theatre and films interested her, and she idolized cowboy star William S. Hart. In the tiny theatre Dr Hepburn had built for her in the backyard, Kate dramatized Uncle Tom's Cabin, casting it with neighbourhood children. 'I wouldn't play Eva because Eva was too good. I played Topsy – and as there was a little girl in the neighbourhood who I wanted to get even with, I chose her for Eva – as Topsy played all the mean tricks on her.'

Up to the age of twelve, Kate was an uncomplicated, energetic, fun-loving, freckled tomboy. But then something happened that altered her character overnight, and indirectly contributed to the kind of actress and woman she was to become.

Left: *Such devoted sisters. Kate (left) with Marion (centre) and Peggy, her virtual double, at the Hepburn family home in 1940.*

Right: *Kit Hepburn flanked by her daughters, Marion (left) and Peggy, at the Radio City première of Kate's new picture,* Alice Adams *(1935).*

2

'Self-conscious Beauty!'

My father had been disgusted and heartsick over the fact that I wanted to act. Thought it a silly profession, closely allied to streetwalking. That I had developed into a cheap show-off and that I was entering a shabby profession which was based on youth and looks.

Kate and her brother Tom were virtually inseparable. He joined her in all her home theatricals. He played the banjo, loved to sing, and wrote some songs of his own. He was a good athlete and student, and his father was making plans for him to enter Yale as a medical student. On Tuesday 29 March 1920, during the Easter holidays, Mrs Hepburn took her two eldest children to New York, where they stayed with a family friend. Brother and sister saw Pavlova dance, explored Greenwich Village, Fifth Avenue and Central Park together, and went to see a play based on Mark Twain's *A Connecticut Yankee in King Arthur's Court*, in which a scene of a hanging plainly impressed Tom.

The next morning, Kate went upstairs to the studio attic to wake Tom, because they were getting the 10.20 from Grand Central back to Hartford. She got no reply when she called him. She screamed when she entered the bedroom and saw her brother's body suspended from a noose made from a torn bedsheet which had been placed around a beam. She frantically cut Tom down and lay him on the bed. Kate, who knew he was dead, was holding her brother in her arms when the doctor arrived fifteen minutes later. Tom had been dead for five hours.

Strangely, there was already a history of suicide on both sides of the family – Dr Hepburn's brother, and Mrs Hepburn's father and uncle. Kate remembered standing on the boat crossing the Hudson going to a crematorium in New Jersey with Tom's body, and seeing her mother crying. 'I'd never seen my mother cry before. And I never saw her cry again.'

Dr Hepburn believed that it was not suicide but a stunt that had gone horribly wrong. The *New York Times* ran a headline the next day: MYSTERY IN SUICIDE OF SURGEON'S SON. FATHER SAYS SON'S HANGING WAS BOYISH STUNT. Whatever the reasons, the tragedy had a severe and long-lasting

Kate as seen in her graduate year in the 1928 Bryn Mawr yearbook, far more at ease with herself than when she arrived at the college.

effect on Kate. A depression set in her, her schoolwork suffered and she found the company of her peers even more difficult. 'I felt isolated. I knew something that the girls did not know: tragedy.'

Because Kate had become a bitter, edgy, moody girl, she was taken out of school and given a tutor, Gradually, she attempted to replace or become her late brother. She spoke of taking up medical studies as Tom might have done and, knowing how much Tom's sporting prowess had pleased her father, she worked hard to equal his achievements. She became excellent at golf, her father's favourite pastime, coming second in the Connecticut Women's Open at fifteen. She won a junior ice-skating championship, and was a good tennis player and a competent swimmer and diver. Many of these athletic abilities were convincingly on display in *Pat and Mike* some decades later.

Kate was not much of a student – she flunked Latin, and had no notion of physics and chemistry. It became clear that becoming a doctor was out of the question, and for a time it seemed as if she would never pass college entrance exams at all. Her parents, however, were determined that she should obtain a degree in some field of study. After a crash course with private tutors, Kate arrived at Bryn Mawr College, her mother's alma mater, at the age of seventeen, totally undisciplined scholastically and with very few social graces. The other girls at the college found it difficult to warm to this oddball, snooty young woman. Kate took showers after midnight when the rest of the dormitory was asleep, bathed in the campus fountain and then rolled herself dry on the grass and once, during a blizzard, went out on to a roof in the nude, allowing herself to be covered with snow.

This exhibitionism might possibly be interpreted as a defence mechanism to conceal her feelings of inadequacy when dealing with girls of her own age. She made no effort to make friends, and had none.

Kate used to eat in her room as much as possible

to avoid going into the dining room. 'In the early part of the semester, I had gone into the dining room... I was dressed in a French blue flared skirt which buttoned up the front with big white buttons – and an Iceland blue and white sweater popular at the time. I certainly did not consider myself beautiful. I was just painfully self-conscious. To my horror, I heard a voice – a New York voice – from the vicinity of where I was supposed to sit: "Self-conscious beauty!" I nearly dropped dead... That year I never went back into that dining room.'

Kate was a poor student, cutting classes regularly, though she especially envied one girl her scholarship. 'I'd go to the library to study and sit next to her. I could hear the wheels whirring in her head. I was insanely jealous, and so, naturally, I loved her.' In her

The barefoot Pandora rests during rehearsals for the May Day college production of John Lyly's The Woman in the Moon.

sophomore year, the dean sent Dr Hepburn a letter suggesting that his daughter drop out of school.

'If I had a patient who was sick,' he replied, 'I wouldn't release him from the hospital.'

What kept her going was the dream of becoming an actress, although when she confided this to a friend, she received the reply, 'You! An actress? You're too skinny and funny-looking!' Unfazed, Kate studied night and day, aware that she would not be eligible for campus dramatics unless her grades improved greatly. They did, and she appeared as a leading man in A. A. Milne's *The Truth about Blayds*, and as Pandora in John Lyly's *The Woman in the Moon*, performed during the traditional May Day celebrations at the college. Barefoot and bare-armed, dressed in a white flowing gown, her red hair loose and blowing madly, Kate made a striking impression. However, her father, whose approval mattered beyond anyone else's, told her 'that all he could see in that performance were the soles of my dirty feet getting blacker and blacker. And my freckled face getting redder and redder.'

Kate's performance gained her a letter of introduction to Edwin H. Knopf, a young theatrical producer who was preparing a season of summer stock in Baltimore. Unfortunately, she was told there was no place for her in the season, and returned to college. But, the following year, on the eve of her graduation, Knopf offered her the part of a lady-in-waiting to Mary Boland in *The Czarina*.

At first, Mary Boland was dismayed by the skinny, red-haired, freckle-faced girl in the wings. She felt Kate's eyes burningly turned on her during rehearsals, and demanded that Knopf have her taken away. But when Boland saw her in a ball dress, she was surprised. 'The ugly duckling became a swan – it was incredible! I never saw anything like that eager girl, so proud to walk across a stage she seemed to be borne up by light.'

When Kate left the Knopf stock company, she

An unusual cheesecake pose from Kate at the beginning of her career – she never took kindly to this sort of thing.

headed for New York in search of an acting coach. She chose Frances Robinson-Duff, an imposing, white-haired woman, with whom Ina Claire, Helen Hayes and other great Broadway stars had studied. She had a classroom on the top floor of an East 62nd Street townhouse. 'I distinctly remember the day she came to me,' recalled Miss Robinson-Duff. 'It was raining. She had run up the stairs. She burst in the door, unannounced, and flung herself on the settee. Rain from her red hair and down her nose. She sat in a dripping huddle and stared. "I want to be an actress!" she explained. "I want to learn everything!"'

At the same time, Kate was being pursued by a young man whom she had met at a Bryn Mawr dance. Ludlow Ogden Smith was the son of wealthy parents, educated at exclusive boarding schools and a graduate of the University of Grenoble. Twenty-nine in 1928, tall and lean, 'Luddy', as Kate always called him, had a degree in industrial engineering that he never used, preferring to pursue a career as an insurance broker instead.

Though Kate described him later as 'an odd-looking man – dark hair, dark eyes far apart. He was foreign-looking. Pink cheeks. An odd nose, long with a hump in it. A long mouth, full-lipped', he possessed a quality of sophistication that she found attractive. In Luddy, Kate gained an attentive and elegant escort, an amusing companion, a sympathetic friend and a man who would never stand in the way of her career. She saw a great deal of him as she prepared for the role of the secretary in Knopf's New York production of *The Big Pond*. In fact, she lost her virginity to him. 'Luddy and I were in the apartment [a mutual friend's] and there was the bed and there didn't seem any reason not to... I mean we did it. I didn't object. And that was the end of my virtue. He was my beau from then on.'

About a week before the scheduled opening in Great Neck, Long Island, Knopf fired the leading lady and replaced her by Kate, just like a scene in *Morning Glory*. But unlike the 1933 RKO movie, the novice actress was totally unprepared for the part and terrified by it. Overcome by stage fright, she gave an appalling performance and was fired. Incredibly she was offered more work, in a flop called *These Days* and as understudy to the star, Hope Williams, in Philip Barry's *Holiday*, which had just opened successfully in New Haven. Williams was a popular light comedienne of the Twenties, whose arch mannerisms and boyish appeal may have influenced Kate's development as an actress. Philip Barry, the playwright, was to become a significant force in her career.

Two weeks later, Kate impetuously accepted a proposal of marriage from Luddy. 'If you want to sacrifice the admiration of many men for the criticism of one, go ahead, get married,' her mother had told her. They were married at her parents' West Hartford home on 12 December1928, and went to Bermuda on their honeymoon. But Kate soon realized that, whatever her histrionic abilities, playing a wife for real was a role that was beyond her.

A month after the Broadway production of *Holiday* closed in June 1929, without Kate ever having stepped on stage, she and Luddy crossed to France. Because difficulties arose between them, the vacation was cut short; they returned to New York within two weeks and took up separate residences. By that time *Holiday* was touring and, when Hope Williams took ill one night, Kate finally got the chance to play the role. This time she was more than adequate. Ten years later, now a glamorous movie star, she was able to make the part her own in George Cukor's dazzling screen version.

Although she got a few good reviews on the road in *Death Takes a Holiday*, in which she played Grazia, a young girl in love with Death, in the personification of Prince Sirki, a handsome man, one critic referred to her as 'a new girl looking for all the world like a death's head, with a metallic voice' and another thought her 'hoydenish and gaunt'. She was subsequently fired and, according to her brutally candid father, 'They were absolutely right. You are carrying on on that stage. You are galumphing there like a maniac. Who's going to believe that my daughter, a big healthy girl like you, could fall in love with death? With death, for God's sakes!'

After a few more roles in summer stock, at the time when Kate felt her career was not going anywhere, she was spotted by theatre producer Gilbert Miller, who offered her the choice role of Leslie Howard's mistress in a Philip Barry play called *The Animal Kingdom* that he was bringing into New York. Rehearsals began in Boston, but Kate and Howard did not get on from the beginning. He hated her 'outrageous posturings' and 'insufferable bossiness'. She thought Howard disliked her because, at five foot seven, she was taller than him.

'I remember one hideous moment when I said, "What would you like me to do here, Mr Howard?" And he answered, "I really don't give a damn what you do, my dear."'

Howard began to put pressure on Miller to have Kate removed, and she was replaced after the Pittsburgh opening. Devastated, she rang Philip Barry to complain about her treatment. When she asked him why she had been fired, to Kate's chagrin, the playwright replied, 'Well, to be brutally frank, you weren't very good.' This from a man, whose play *The Philadelphia Story*, written with her in mind, would later resuscitate her career, and who would become a great friend.

Then, in the vicissitudinous manner that typifies Kate's career, she was offered the part of Antiope, the energetic and athletic Queen of the Amazons (ideal casting) in Julian Thompson's *The Warrior's Husband*, loosely based on *Lysistrata*, which opened at the Morosco Theatre in March 1932. From the moment she entered in her short-skirted Greek costume, leaping spectacularly down a treacherous twenty-step stairway three steps at a time, a stuffed deer with an arrow in its back wrapped around her shoulders, she staked her claim to stardom.

The critics raved and Hollywood talent scouts started nosing around. 'Nobody ever noticed me until

Antiope, Queen of the Amazons, in The Warrior's Husband *at the Morosco Theatre in 1932, the stage role that brought Kate to the attention of Hollywood.*

scene from *Holiday*, which she had understudied for six months. She played it with desperate earnestness, miserably conscious of the camera, and overemphasizing all the wrong words.

As fate would have it, David O. Selznick was at that time struggling with the casting of the film version of Clemence Dane's *A Bill of Divorcement* at RKO, to be directed by George Cukor. Norma Shearer and Irene Dunne were among those considered for the key role of the daughter. To Cukor's astonishment, Selznick suddenly decided to cast his current girlfriend, 'a pretty little blonde *ingénue*'. Cukor, disgusted, threatened to quit. Hayward got word of the problem at RKO and persuaded Cukor to see Kate's test.

'She was quite unlike anybody I had ever seen... I thought, I suppose right away, "She's too odd. It won't work." But at one moment in a very emotional scene, she picked up a glass. The camera focused on her back. There was an enormous feeling, a weight about the manner in which she picked up the glass.'

Cukor had a terrible time persuading Selznick even to look at the test. He got top screenwriter Adela Rogers St John to back him up. Kate had just opened in a new play, *The Bride the Sun Shines on*, in summer stock when she received a telegram from Hayward telling her that not only would RKO meet her $1500-a-week demand, she was to leave for California immediately to appear opposite John Barrymore in her first film.

I was in a leg show,' was Kate's comment. Halfway through the run of eighty-three performances, a Hollywood agent named Leland Hayward began to court her as a client. He thought that her vivacious personality and striking appearance would best be displayed on film, and he saw her as star potential. He talked to Paramount and they made a small offer for her services. Kate turned them down. With a shrewdness beyond her years and station, Kate insisted Hayward set $1500 a week as her price. RKO picked up the bait and asked her to take a screen test in New York. She chose a

3

'My Star Will Never Set'

*Everyone thought I was bold and
fearless, and even arrogant... but
inwardly I was always quaking... I've
never cared about how afraid I may have
been inside — I've always done what I
thought I should.*

In July 1932, Luddy saw Kate and her actress friend Laura Harding off to Hollywood on the Super Chief. In order to avoid the press, she stepped off the train in Pasadena, believing she looked quite elegant in an ill-fitting grey silk suit with a matching pancake hat, which she described as 'a sort of grey-blue straw dish upside down on my head'. To Leland Hayward and partner Myron Selznick, David's older brother, who had driven out from Los Angeles to meet her, her outfit appeared more bizarre than stylish. She also had a swollen eye from having got steel filings embedded in it on the train. Her hair was drawn tightly back, screwed into a casual knot and tucked under the band of her hat.

'This is what David's paying $1500 a week for?' Myron gasped.

Kate and Laura were then taken to the very smart Château Marmont Hotel above Sunset Boulevard. The next morning Kate arrived at the studio to be greeted by George Cukor, whose first reaction in seeing this 'boa constrictor on a fast' was even worse than Myron's. He thought he had made the most horrible mistake.

When Cukor showed her the sketches for her costumes for the film, Kate peered at them through red eyes and said, 'They're no good! I want my clothes designed by someone like Chanel.'

This got Cukor's dander up. 'Considering the way you look, I can hardly take your judgement seriously.'

'I thought these clothes were pretty fancy. I paid a great deal for them.'

'Well, they're terrible. You look ghastly. I think any woman who would wear such an outfit outside a bathroom wouldn't know what clothes are. Now what do you think of that?'

'You win. Pick out the clothes you want,' Kate acknowledged, extending her hand for Cukor to shake.

Cukor, then thirty-three, was a portly, bespectacled homosexual with

Kate made over by Hollywood in the Garbo mould. It took some time for them to exploit her own very special personality.

whom Kate was to become firm friends for life. He was also to prove one of her most sympathetic directors.

Kate's next studio appointment was with the RKO publicity department. The meeting lasted barely five minutes, during which time she announced that her private life was her own and that she did not believe in publicity. Nobody had any idea that she was married.

The make-up and hairdressing departments also threw up their hands in despair after an encounter with the studio's new acquisition. Kate told them she could do her own face and hair better than they could. Cukor agreed that her natural looks should be preserved but insisted the freckles and frizzy hair had to go. (For years heavy make-up blotted out her freckles on screen and they were removed from all stills.)

At the first encounter with her co-star in *A Bill of Divorcement*, former matinée idol John Barrymore, a notorious womanizer and drinker, he walked unsteadily over to Kate and peered into her inflamed eyes. 'I also hit the bottle occasionally, my dear. But I have a perfect disguise. You see this little phial of eyedrops? When I use it, it clears up the inflammation right away. People think I've been cold sober.'

'But, Mr Barrymore, I have a cinder in my eye!'

'That's what they all say, my dear.'

Later, Barrymore invited her to his dressing room and, without warning, threw all his clothes off. Kate was astonished and backed against the wall.

'My dear, any young girl would be thrilled to make love to the great John Barrymore.'

'Not me,' Kate said in terror. 'My father doesn't want me to make babies.'

On another occasion, Barrymore was said to have pinched her behind. 'If you do that again,' she said, 'I'm going to stop acting.'

'I wasn't aware you had started, my dear,' Barrymore snapped.

Kate enjoying the material benefits of stardom in her 1952 Bugatti, although she was never a showy person.

Above: *One of the many
vampish publicity stills to
which Kate had to submit in
her early years in Hollywood.*

Right: *Her strong
personality yet to emerge,
Kate is glamorized and
freckleless but instantly
recognizable in 1933.*

*Rapidly making up on the set
of* Sylvia Scarlett, *in
which George Cukor directed
Kate for the third time.*

*On the set of her second
triumph,* Morning Glory,
*in her infamous dungarees,
the cause of much disquiet in
the publicity department.
Director Lowell Sherman is
the dark-haired man in
the background.*

Kate denies this story. 'Barrymore never criticized me. He just shoved me before the cameras. He taught me all that could be poured into one greenhorn in that short a time.'

The press, having got wind that a new star was on the horizon, hung around the lot. The studio was dismayed because Kate would appear between scenes in her old dungarees, hardly befitting the glamorous image they were trying to disseminate. When she was asked to stopped wearing them, she refused. One day, she returned to her dressing room to find the offending garment gone. Thereupon, she walked through the lot in her underpants. It did the trick and, to Kate's delight, she was given back her pet dungarees.

Selznick's first reaction to the rushes of *A Bill of Divorcement* may have been 'Ye gods, that horse face!', but Cukor had no such qualms. Her freshness and directness made her ideal for the role of Sydney Fairfield, the daughter of a shell-shocked World War I victim (Barrymore) who escapes from an asylum, returning home on the very day his wife (Billie Burke), who has divorced him, is to marry again. His daughter, who also has plans to marry, gives up her own future to care for her father.

Although Kate was rather awkward in her movements and talked rapidly in a grating voice in the early scenes, it was still obvious to audiences that they were in the presence of a unique personality. Growing in confidence as the picture moves towards its climax, she conveys a tenderness mixed with aggressiveness that seems modern today in contrast with Barrymore's rather dated, theatrical style. It is doubtful, however, that anyone imagined that *A Bill of Divorcement* was the launching pad of the career of one of the greatest of screen actresses. As the actor Roddy McDowell has said, 'We take Katharine Hepburn for granted now. The sort of bravery, the wonderful lithe figure. But when she first appeared on the screen, they said, "What is this?" She defied

the law of possibility. She was a total original.'

The director Rouben Mamoulian once commented that few Hollywood actresses had a truly individual manner of walking. He mentioned Garbo, Cyd Charisse and Kate, who in her very first film demonstrated that distinctive cross between a stride and a lope, at the same time both stylish and gauche.

Before the film was previewed, Kate and Luddy decided they should go to Europe to see if they could make something of their marriage. Also, as Kate had not seen the final cut, she preferred to be far away at the opening in case she had made a fool of herself. The memory of her recent sackings and severe criticisms in the theatre was still fresh in her mind.

She need not have worried. *A Bill of Divorcement* was generally well received, but Kate's personal reviews were wonderful. The *New Yorker* called her 'half Botticelli page and half bobbed-hair bandit', and the *Journal-American* claimed she had 'flamed like opal, half-demon, half-madonna'. As a result, Selznick got RKO to pick up Kate's option.

Kate and Luddy were in Vienna when she received a telegram from Hayward urging her to return to New York. He had negotiated a new RKO contract, and the studio had a film planned for her, entitled *Three Came Unarmed*. When she arrived in New York, she denied to reporters that she was

The débutante screen actress sharing a dramatic scene in A Bill of Divorcement *(1932) with Henry Stephenson (far left), John Barrymore (left) and Billie Burke.*

married, and answered a fan magazine's question of 'Have you any children?' with 'Yes, two white and three coloured.'

For the next four decades, Kate waged a vigorous battle to protect her privacy. She has said that on arrival in Hollywood she divided the world into two spheres; one was her private domain, the other was 'enemy territory'. She rarely went to parties or premières, and never dated Hollywood's eligible bachelors. Kate saw few people outside those of George Cukor's circle. At Cukor's famous Sunday lunches, however, she met a glittering array of film and literary celebrities, including Greta Garbo, her favourite actress.

At one of George Cukor's celebrated Sunday lunches for artists and intellectuals, with writers Hugh Walpole (left) and Roland Leigh.

Kate's clothes were also cause for comment in the Hollywood community. Apart from the gowns worn for glossy publicity stills, she had a few dresses for public appearances – many of them designed by Elizabeth Hawes – which somehow made her look dowdy. In private, she nearly always wore trousers.

Three Came Unarmed, which was to have paired her with Joel McCrea, was abandoned because of script problems. On the other hand, RKO had just purchased Gilbert Frankau's novel *Christopher Strong* and the role of the daredevil aviatrix Lady Cynthia Darrington seemed tailor-made for Kate. The story tells how the record-breaking pilot falls in love with Sir Christopher Strong (Colin Clive), a married man, becomes pregnant and kills herself by pulling off her oxygen mask while breaking the altitude record at 30,000 feet.

To Kate's delight, Selznick hired Dorothy Arzner, one of Hollywood's few women directors. But she was soon disillusioned. Although they developed a mutual respect, their relationship remained cool, distant and competitive. At one stage in the shooting, Arzner threatened to quit unless Kate stopped interfering with her direction. All this did not help the film, which turned out to be a creaky vehicle that never got off the ground, and it bombed at the box office. However, Kate, stalking around in aviator's gear, and mooning and swooning in the love scenes, laid the basis of her career-long screen persona – independent, intelligent, intrepid but, at the same time, extremely sensitive. She was still too self-conscious and fussy, and her voice was too shrill, but she held the eye. Brendan Gill, writing of Kate's early heroines, pronounced that 'they would make love after marriage and then only with a certain fastidious reluctance, nostrils flaring'. She plainly got up the noses of many a macho male, and it is ironic that the film's title is not the name of the leading character, but that of her rather stiff lover.

Soon after completing *Christopher Strong*, Kate was in the office of RKO producer Pandro Berman and happened to come across a script lying on his desk, which she idly began to read. 'I thought, "Oh, my God, that's the most wonderful part ever written for anyone."' She slipped the

As aviatrix Lady Cynthia Darrington in Dorothy Arzner's Christopher Strong *(1933), a few years before Kate was taught to fly by Howard Hughes.*

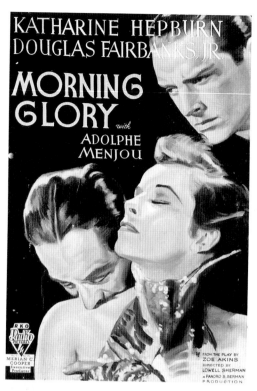

Adolphe Menjou demonstrating a vampire kiss on Kate as Douglas Fairbanks Jr looks on – RKO's idea of a come-on.

manuscript into her bag and took it home. After finishing it, she returned it in person to a nonplussed Berman, announcing, 'This is what I'd like to do next.'

Although Zoë Akins' script of her own play *Morning Glory* had been scheduled for Constance Bennett, Kate forced the studio to give her the part of the struggling young actress Eva Lovelace. One of the reasons for her hankering to play the role was its proximity to her own experiences.

Eva finds it difficult to get an acting job, until a friend and mentor takes her to a party given for a Broadway star, Rita Vernon. At the party she drinks too much champagne and, without warning, starts acting Juliet's balcony scene for the guests. However unconventional, her performance demonstrates her acting ability, and she becomes understudy to the star, taking over from her triumphantly when Vernon walks out of the show. 'Now you belong to no man. You belong to Broadway,' the producer (Adolphe Menjou) tells her.

Eva Lovelace was the role that really made Kate into a movie star. As a character burning with ambition, she was refreshing,

earnest and heart-breaking, even though she tottered on the edges of being embarrassing. When she said in her distinctive nasal voice, 'My star will never set,' it was not difficult to believe!

Within a week of the picture's opening, Kate knew that she had triumphed. Most of the reviews were ecstatic. The *New York Herald Tribune* commented that 'the striking and inescapably fascinating Miss Hepburn proves pretty conclusively in her new film that her fame in the cinema is not a mere flash across the screen... It is Miss Hepburn who makes *Morning Glory* something to be seen.'

As usual, there were a few detractors who found her too mannered, and she first began to be impersonated on radio and in nightclubs. As imitation is the greatest form of flattery, Kate knew she had really arrived.

Mean, moody and magnificent in a publicity still from the early 1930s.

Douglas Fairbanks Jr playing Romeo to Kate's Juliet in a scene from Morning Glory *(1933). It was a role Fairbanks would have liked to play to her in real life.*

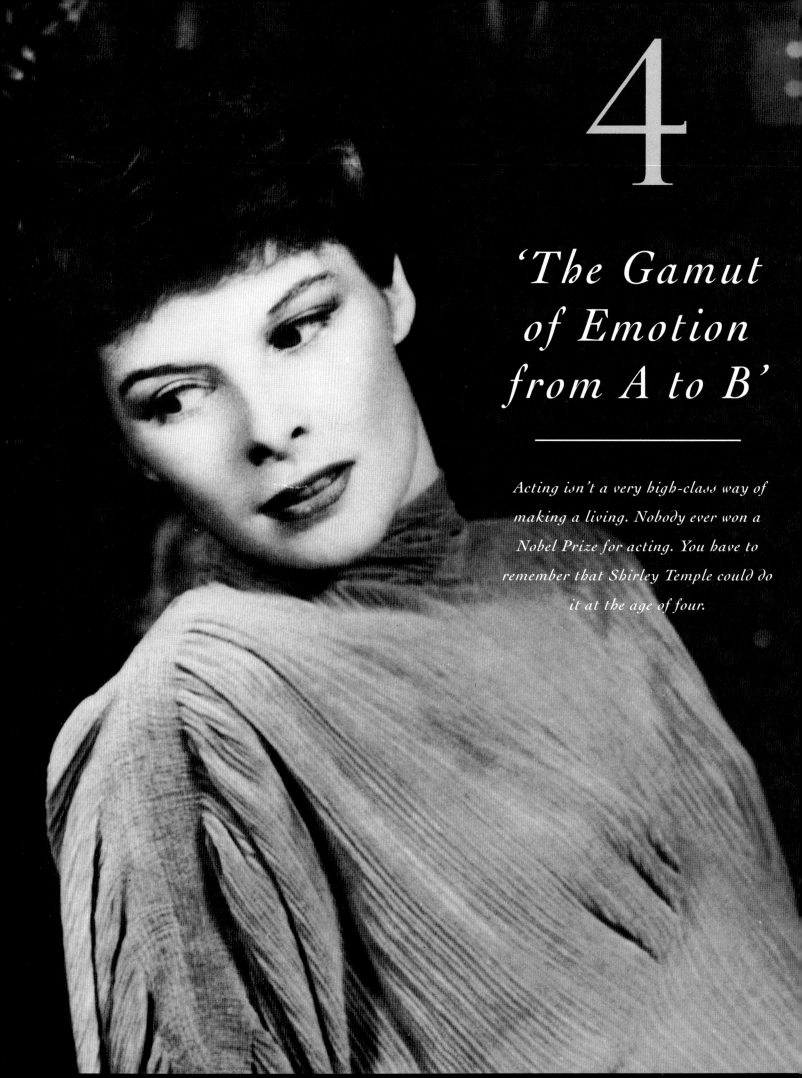

4

'The Gamut of Emotion from A to B'

Acting isn't a very high-class way of making a living. Nobody ever won a Nobel Prize for acting. You have to remember that Shirley Temple could do it at the age of four.

During the making of *Morning Glory*, Douglas Fairbanks Jr, who was Kate's romantic lead, tried for days to get her to go out with him. Like many of her other leading men, after initially disliking her, he was completely captivated. Finally she accepted but, halfway through dinner, complained of a headache. Fairbanks drove her home, but didn't drive straight off, watching as she entered the house. 'Suddenly,' he recalled, 'the front door flew open and Kate came running out. Another car I hadn't noticed was hidden further up the driveway under some trees. She hopped in, and I saw a man at the wheel. They drove right past me without noticing me. She

Accompanied by Douglas Fairbanks Jr, an undelighted Kate is seen leaving producer Jess Lasky's Santa Monica home in December 1933, just after Fairbanks' divorce from Joan Crawford.

was laughing happily, her hair blowing over her face.'

The man at the wheel was Kate's agent, Leland Hayward, who had fallen in love with his client. Hayward, a man who loved and respected intelligent women, had married, divorced and remarried Lola Gibbs, a Texan beauty who was also an aviatrix and had taught him to fly. He was handsome, charming and impeccably tailored; he piloted his own plane to and from New York, and drove a Rolls-Royce.

'I could see very quickly that I suited Leland perfectly,' Kate remembered. 'I liked to eat at home and go to bed early. He liked to eat out and go to bed late. So he had a drink when I had dinner and then off he'd go. Back at midnight. Perfect friendship... Life with Leland had no problems... I don't remember any fights. We just enjoyed – enjoyed – enjoyed.'

But they were still both married and couldn't be seen alone together in public. Nevertheless, he would visit her often at her Cold Water Canyon house. It was while working on her next film, *Little Women*, directed by George Cukor, that Kate had to cope with her deep feelings for Leland, the responsibility of perhaps causing him to divorce his wife and marry her, and the issue of her own probable divorce from Luddy.

There had been a lot of Kate in *A Bill of Divorcement*, in the impatient and anti-establishment young woman, and in the idealistic New

Top Hollywood agent Leland Hayward, an extremely important figure in both Kate's personal and her public life.

Opposite: Kate beginning to look more like herself as a veteran of three feature films in 1933.

Ideally cast as Jo March in George Cukor's LittleWomen (1933), one of Kate's most cherished parts.

A hoop-skirted Kate taking time off from the filming of Little Women to watch others at work while being photographed from below.

England actress in *Morning Glory*, but in *Little Women* she was able to play an emancipated woman modelled on her mother. The Louisa May Alcott novel had always been a special favourite of Kate's, but Cukor, who had considered the book 'a story that little girls read', was startled when he read it for the first time. He found it a 'very strong-minded story, full of character and a wonderful picture of New England family life'; he felt that Kate was born to play Jo March because 'she's tender and odd and

During a break in Little Women, *Kate lunches with George Cukor, her favourite director and one of her closest friends.*

funny, sweet and yet tough, intensely loyal, with an enormous sense of family and all of Jo's burning ambition, and at heart a pure, clean simplicity and firmness'.

There was, however, the occasional contretemps between star and director during the shooting. Walter Plunkett had made beautiful costumes out of authentic period material, and Kate was warned that they couldn't be replaced if she spoiled them. One shot required her to run up a flight of stairs carrying a dish of ice cream. Swept away by the scene, Kate forgot the warning and spilled ice cream on her skirt. Furious, Cukor slapped her face in front of the entire cast and crew – an insult that Kate accepted stoically, out of her respect for Cukor.

In this best of the three screen versions of *Little Women*, Kate gives a penetrating and subtly moving

Barefoot Kate trying to convince as an illiterate mountain girl in Spitfire *(1934) – audiences failed to respond.*

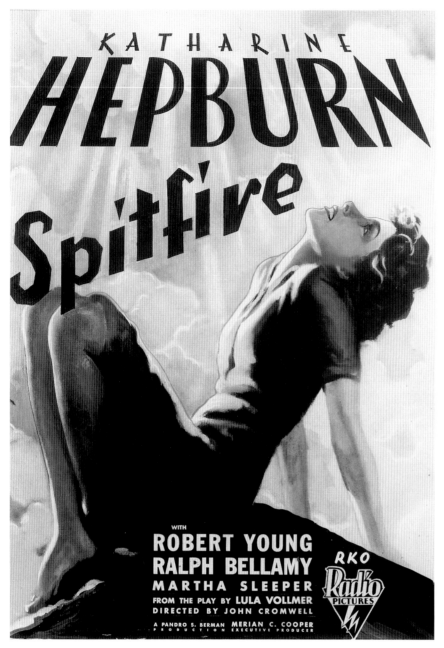

Kate's attempt to broaden her range resulted in one of her many flops in the 1930s.

Massingham and Murray MacDonald, to be produced by Jed Harris, the wizard of the Broadway theatre. Harris thought that Kate's current box-office popularity would help secure his investment. But RKO would only release her to do the play if she made another picture for them first. Perhaps she accepted *Spitfire* in order to prove that she could play a character other than blue-blooded East Coast types. It turned out to be a severe miscalculation. Although Kate made a spirited attempt at the role of a wild, quick-tempered, illiterate mountain girl who believes she has the gift in her hands to cure the lame, her natural elegance and breeding kept showing through the portrayal. The *New Yorker* thought 'her artistry does not extend to the primitive or uncouth'. The public did not appreciate it either, and *Spitfire* flopped.

On the personal side, Kate's pride was hurt when Leland Hayward began a relationship with Margaret Sullavan, a new young star. Jed Harris, too, had had an affair with Sullavan. In fact, Kate had no idea that the Harris-Sullavan affair was not quite over, nor that Sullavan had been

portrait of a resolute girl on the edge of womanhood. Beautifully lit, her expressive face is alive with joy, hope and despair.

Little Women was the first of her films to be an enormous box-office hit, and her stock stood high in Hollywood. RKO lined up numerous projects for her: Edith Wharton's *The Age of Innocence* and biopics of Sarah Bernhardt, Nell Gwyn and Queen Elizabeth. None of these inspired Kate and, buoyed up by her success in *Little Women*, she made a rash decision to return to the stage.

The play chosen was *The Lake* by Dorothy

Harris's first choice for the role in *The Lake*. With her relationship with Leland threatened, Kate was particularly susceptible to Harris's charm when she arrived in New York, believing that he would dedicate himself to her success in the play because of his respect for her as a stage actress. Nothing could have been further from the truth. He not only resented the fact that Kate, not Sullavan, was playing the role, he thought he had made a serious mistake in casting her.

Harris explained: 'I could see she was hopeless. I fought with her – I begged her to stop posing, striking attitudes, leaning against doorways, putting a limp hand to her forehead, to stop being a big movie star and feel the lines, feel the character. I was trying the impossible, to make an artificial showcase of an artificial star, and she couldn't handle it.'

But Harris drove her unmercifully. One witness remarked: 'If she turned her head to the left, he didn't like it. If she turned it to the right, he liked it still less.' The director's bullying did not diminish Kate's infatuation for him in the least. On the contrary. During one confrontation, she threw her arms around his neck and cried, 'I could have loved you so.'

In a way, Harris's instincts were correct. The role of a blighted young society woman whose husband drowns in a lake on the first day of their marriage, and suffers tremendous guilt because she loved a married man instead of him, would have been more suitable for Sullavan's delicate talents. The character is not a rebel, and Kate's quality was her strength.

The Lake was quite well received when it opened in Washington DC on 17 December 1933, but Harris, feeling Kate was not ready for Broadway, implored Kate to tour before going to New York. Kate stubbornly refused, arguing it would harm her career.

'My dear, the only interest I have in you is the money I can make out of you,' Harris told her.

Stunned, Kate stammered, 'How much will it cost you to open in New York?'.

'How much have you got?'

She opened her chequebook and said, 'I've got exactly $15,461 and 67 cents.'

'OK, I'll take that.'

Kate wrote the cheque for the full amount and the next day the company left for New York. On opening night, 26 December, the entire Hepburn family was there, plus Noël Coward, Gertrude Lawrence, Leland Hayward, George S. Kaufman, Amelia Earhart and Dorothy Parker. Kate started at such a fast pace that her timing was thrown off and her voice grew steadily more frenzied in decibel and pitch. It didn't help that she had to utter lines like 'The calla lilies are in bloom again. Such a strange flower. I carried them on my wedding day. And now I place them here, in memory of someone who is dead.'

Noël Coward came back stage and said, 'You mucked it up, but that happens to all of us. You'll get roasted. But keep at it. You'll find the way.' The next day, Dorothy Parker's barbed remark appeared in the press: 'Go to the Martin Beck Theatre and see Katharine Hepburn run the gamut of emotion from A to B.' This still famous quote was an albatross that hung around Kate's neck for years. To her relief, *The Lake* closed after fifty-five performances.

At the same time, Mrs Hepburn was courting notoriety after appearing on the stand of the House Caucus Room in Washington in passionate argument for a bill permitting the dissemination of birth-control information by physicians. An interview in the *New York Times* carried the headline STAR'S MOTHER FIRM IN STAND. Another event added to Kate's anxiety. When Margaret Sullavan married William Wyler, whom she had known for only a few weeks, Leland Hayward took the news harder than Kate would have wished.

With all this weighing upon her, Kate decided to take a trip to Europe, ostensibly to pick up her award for Best Actress in *Little Women* at Cannes. The day she sailed on the *Paris*, her career, seemingly in the doldrums, received a boost. She was informed that she had won the Best Actress Oscar for *Morning Glory*.

Unable to attend the ceremony, she wrote a telegram saying she didn't believe in acting contests and therefore felt it her duty to refuse the award. Hayward read the wire, tore it up and sent a thank-you note instead. 'He was right,' Kate said years later. 'I was being childish.' But she never picked up any of her four Oscars. 'I'm not proud that I didn't. I just never got round to it.'

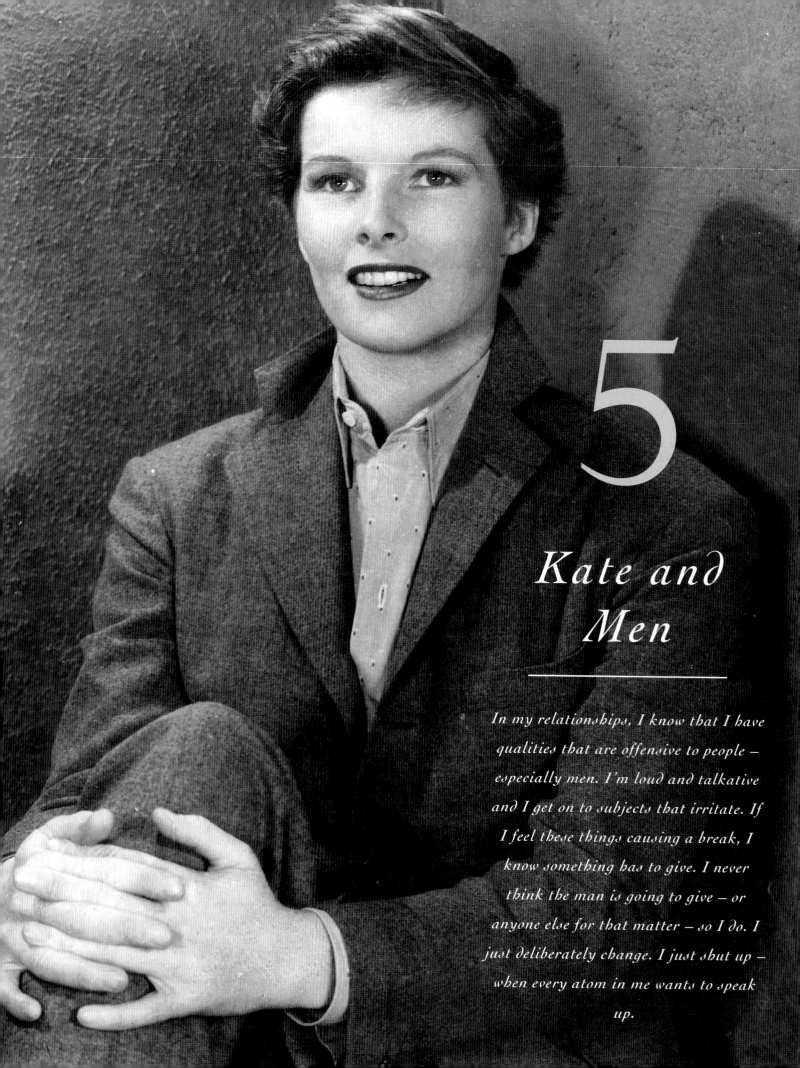

5

Kate and Men

In my relationships, I know that I have
qualities that are offensive to people –
especially men. I'm loud and talkative
and I get on to subjects that irritate. If
I feel these things causing a break, I
know something has to give. I never
think the man is going to give – or
anyone else for that matter – so I do. I
just deliberately change. I just shut up –
when every atom in me wants to speak
up.

The trip to France lasted a mere four days, before Kate returned on the same ship. On the voyage home she met Ernest Hemingway, with whom she strolled the decks, dined and argued enthusiastically. Despite her marriage to Ludlow Ogden Smith, her affair with Leland Hayward and her attraction to Jed Harris, all three urban sophisticates, Kate was drawn more to rugged men's men like Hemingway, George Stevens, John Ford, Howard Hughes and, of course, Spencer Tracy.

From New York she went to Mexico, where she obtained a divorce from Luddy. Reporters on her return asked about her mother's work in birth control. 'Mother has accomplished a great deal. I detest the newspaper references to her as Katharine Hepburn's mother. My

Kate posing for photographers aboard the SS Paris on her return from Europe in April 1934.

mother is important. I am not.' When asked about whether she would now marry her agent, she replied, 'I won't discuss my personal affairs ever. They wouldn't be personal if I made them public.'

Curiously, once divorced from Luddy, she missed him. They even shared a house from time to time, and could count on each other's friendship. 'Dear Luddy. He would always meet the train or the plane when I returned from Hollywood. He would drive me to Fenwick or Hartford. We were separated. Then we were divorced – in Yucatan, Mexico. I didn't think that the divorce was any good, but I thought it made our position clear. Luddy took another apartment. He continued to do for me any and every possible kindness.'

Afterwards Kate returned to Hollywood to complete her RKO contract, making Technicolor tests for Joan of Arc, but the film was dropped. There were plans for Kate to co-star with Garbo in the Eugene O'Neill drama *Mourning Becomes Electra* at MGM, but Louis B. Mayer turned the idea down. Disappointed, Kate rejected various scripts, including an adaptation of J. M. Barrie's *The Little Minister*. However, when Kate learned that Margaret Sullavan, her rival for Leland Hayward's love, had been approached for the part, she changed her mind. 'I really didn't want to play it until I heard another actress was desperate for that role,' Kate later admitted. 'Then, of course, it became the most important thing in the world for me that I should get it. Several of my parts in those days I fought for just to take them from someone who needed them.'

Set in Scotland in 1840, *The Little*

The martyr that never was. Kate making a Technicolor screen test for the role of George Bernard Shaw's Saint Joan.

Opposite: 'The handsomest boy of the season.' Kate in a slim disguise in George Cukor's Sylvia Scarlett (1936).

Minister is the story of Lady Babbie, who is democratic at heart and loves to dress up as a gypsy, mingling with the humble weavers of the Scottish valley. She gets involved in the weavers' rebellion against her stern foster father and horrifies the villagers by falling in love with the prim young minister. With a second-league cast and director (Richard Wallace), Kate had to carry the whole picture, which she did to a large extent, creating a sympathetic and attractive non-conformist character. Although *The Little Minister* was perhaps too affected for Depression audiences, it did not fail entirely at the box office; it nevertheless lost $9000, because it was RKO's most expensive film of the year, and the

John Beal in the title role of The Little Minister *(1934), being comforted by Kate under the close eye of director Richard Wallace.*

most expensive in which Kate had appeared. According to Pandro Berman, 'Kate wasn't a movie star. She wasn't going to become a star, either, in the sense that Crawford and Shearer were – actresses able to drag an audience in by their own efforts. She was a hit only in hit pictures; she couldn't save a flop. And she almost invariably chose the wrong vehicles.'

After the completion of *The Little Minister*, Leland Hayward and Kate flew to New York. There they were hounded by reporters, who spread a rumour that they were married, something that the couple never bothered to deny. Both Kate and Leland were free and single, but marriage was not an option Kate ever thought of taking. As she later explained, 'For the independent woman the marriage problem is very great. If she falls in love with a strong man she loses him because she has to concentrate too much on her job. If she falls in love with a weakling, whom she can push around, she always falls out of love with him. A woman just has to have sense enough to handle a man well enough so he'll want to stay with her. How to keep him on a string is almost a full-time job.'

At Christmas in 1934, Leland was suddenly taken ill. Cancer of the prostate was suspected and Kate insisted they fly to West

James Barrie's 'immortal masterpiece' failed to survive in its screen version, which starred Kate in another period role.

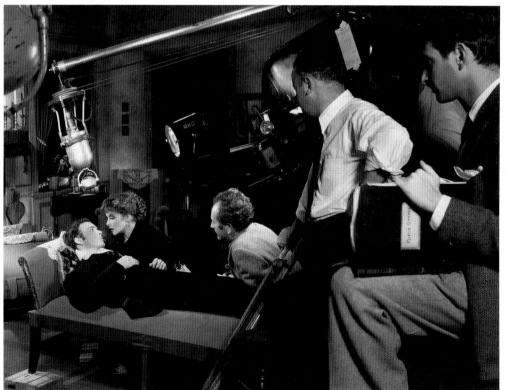

Hartford so that Dr Hepburn could perform the operation required. It was a story that the press found irresistible – 'Movie Star's Doctor Father Operates on Daughter's Fiancé – so reporters descended on the town. One day, when Kate was emerging from her house, flash-bulbs exploded in her face. Incensed, she grabbed the nearest photographer, and threw his camera to the ground. Then she turned and ran back into the house where she was met by her sister Peggy.

Charles Boyer and Kate made beautiful music together as conductor and composer in Break of Hearts *(1935), but the box-office takings sounded a sour note.*

'Where's the shotgun?' she shouted. 'Get it! Get it!' However, before more damage was done, Mrs Hepburn put the photographers to flight with a wire basket.

The operation on Leland was a success and, after a brief recuperation at the Hepburn house, he returned to California. Kate followed soon after, but they saw little of each other, and she was able to concentrate on her work. Unfortunately, her next film, *Break of Hearts*, turned out to be another critical and commercial disaster – and rightly so! Pandro Berman had persuaded Kate to star in this banal melodrama against her wishes. The film is about a temperamental and brilliant conductor (Charles Boyer) married to a struggling composer (Hepburn). When he becomes an alcoholic, she gives up her promising career to help him out of his drunken stupor. Again, as in most of her previous films, here was a woman in her own right, sacrificing herself for a man. During the filming Kate herself was rather smitten with the happily married Boyer and she could be seen, between takes, resting her head on his knee and looking up at him adoringly.

In an effort to save Kate's tarnished reputation, RKO cast her in the title role of *Alice Adams*, based on Booth Tarkington's touching story of small-town life. As Kate's contract had given her first choice of director, she considered George Cukor and William Wyler ideal for the subject. But Cukor was busy on David Copperfield, and William Wyler's marriage to Margaret Sullavan put him out of the running. She was forced to accept thirty-year-old George Stevens, whose only previous features had been routine comedies. Their relationship followed the pattern of so many prior ones, with the pair first being at odds, then gradually becoming attracted to each other.

One of the few happy moments in Break of Hearts, *during the filming of which Kate became briefly enamoured of Charles Boyer.*

GRETA GARBO'S TRUE LIFE STORY

Modern Screen

JANUARY
10
CENTS

THE LARGEST
CIRCULATION
OF ANY SCREEN
MAGAZINE

Earl
Christy

KATHARINE
HEPBURN

CHARLES BOYER TELLS ON HIMSELF!

Left: *Kate depicted as red-headed but unfreckled and green-eyed (hers were actually blue), making the fan-magazine covers, as she continued to do for years to come.*

Right: *Not the most accurate portrait of Kate for the cover of* Picture Play *in May 1933.*

STREET & SMITH'S

PICTURE PLAY

MAY 1933

10 CENTS

KATHARINE HEPBURN

IRVING SINCLAIR

THE STRANGE CASE OF BOB MONTGOMERY

Kate uncomfortably displaying one of Bernard Newman's costumes from Break of Hearts.

Smiling at co-star Fred MacMurray off set on Alice Adams *(1935). Director George Stevens is on MacMurray's left.*

As wallflower Alice Adams, desperately pretending she is the belle of the ball, Kate embarrasses her brother, played by Frank Albertson.

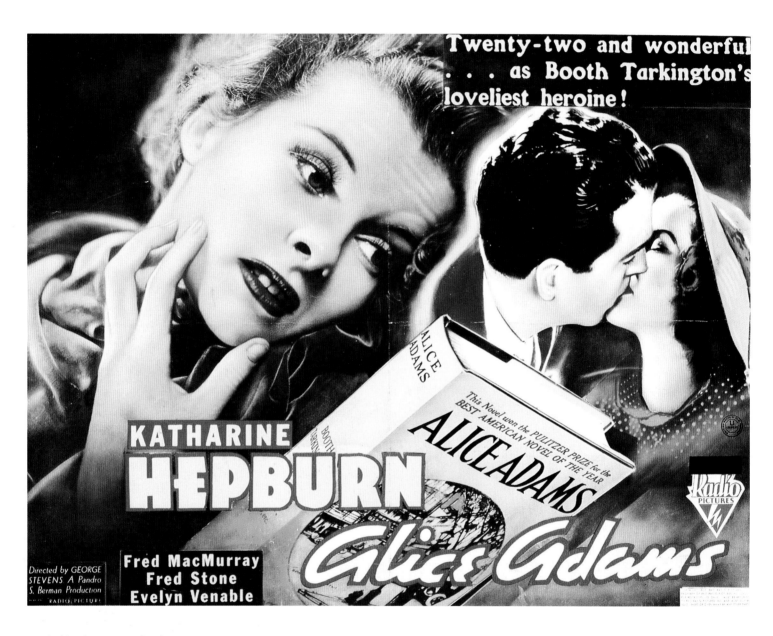

Twenty-two and wonderful
. . . as Booth Tarkington's
loveliest heroine!

KATHARINE HEPBURN

Directed by GEORGE
STEVENS A Pandro
S. Berman Production

**Fred MacMurray
Fred Stone
Evelyn Venable**

This Novel won the PULITZER PRIZE for the
BEST AMERICAN NOVEL OF THE YEAR

ALICE ADAMS

Alice Adams

Radio PICTURES

*The film that gave Kate's
screen career a temporary
boost, as well as putting
director George Stevens in the
first division.*

A lobby card for the film that plunged Kate down to the box-office depths, though it now enjoys cult status.

Kate as the doomed queen Mary Stuart with Fredric March as the Earl of Bothwell in John Ford's fustian drama.

An intense George Stevens directing a scene from Alice Adams as Kate looks on. Director and actress were attracted to each other.

56

Aged twenty-eight, in a publicity still dated 1935, when she was still hankering to play a contemporary American woman.

'A queer feeling.' Brian Aherne fails to understand his emotions when in the presence of a handsome young lad in Sylvia Scarlett.

George Cukor directing a travesty Kate in Sylvia Scarlett, *considered too sophisticated for audiences at the time.*

As a small-town girl snubbed by society because of her father's lack of money and ambition, Alice Adams was a character well-suited to Kate's talents, and she played her with a subtle mixture of acceptance and frustration, idealism and disenchantment, subduing most of her irritating mannerisms. She does have her affected moments, but Kate convinces us that these belong to the character rather than the actress. In the best scenes – when she invites her beau, Fred MacMurray, to a disastrous dinner with her family, or at the ball, anxiously glancing around for a man to ask her to dance – Kate reveals the pain and confusion that comes from rejection. The picture was a hit, and she recovered her good standing in Hollywood. Her next film, *Sylvia Scarlett*, was to undermine it again.

George Cukor had wanted to do *Sylvia Scarlett* for a number of years and gave Kate Compton Mackenzie's book to read, believing her special boyish quality made her perfect for the part. Kate agreed and she and Cukor finally (after much resistance) persuaded Pandro Berman to produce the film. He later called it 'by far the worst picture I ever made, and the greatest catastrophe of Kate's Thirties career'. He added that Cukor and Kate had 'conned me into it and had a script written. I said to them, "Jesus, this is awful, terrible, I don't understand a thing that's going on." I tried to stop them, but they wouldn't be stopped. They were hell-bent, claiming that this was the greatest thing they had ever found.'

Sylvia Scarlett was a daring choice for Kate, an off-beat story of a girl who disguises herself as a boy to help her father, who is a thief and a con man. They meet a crook (Cary Grant) and Sylvia falls in love with an artist (Brian Aherne). He is strangely attracted to her in her boy's disguise, and says, 'I don't know what it is that gives me a queer feeling when I look at you.'

The film, with its references to Shakespeare's travesty roles, was far too sophisticated for general audiences. They complained that they couldn't understand the English accents, especially Cary Grant's cockney, nor were they happy with the ambivalent sexuality, nor the fact that Kate masquerades as a boy through most of the action. Nevertheless, the public had accepted Greta Garbo in drag in *Queen Christina* two years before, though Kate's remarkable androgynous portrayal was more convincing. The *New York Herald Tribune* thought 'the dynamic Miss Hepburn is the handsomest boy of the season' and *Time* declared, '*Sylvia Scarlett* reveals the interesting fact that Katharine Hepburn is better looking as a boy than a woman.'

The picture was Kate's first of four pairings with Cary Grant, a seemingly perfect coming-together of two aristocrats of the cinema. But, as Kate's partnership with Spencer Tracy confirms, chalk and cheese can often be a better combination. Of his first meeting with Kate, Grant commented, 'She was this slip of a woman, skinny, and I never liked skinny women. But she had this thing, this air, you might call it, the most totally magnetic woman I'd ever seen, and probably have ever seen since. You had to look at her, you had to listen to her, there was no escaping her. But it wasn't just the beauty, it was the style. She's incredibly down to earth. She can see right through the nonsense in life. She cares, but about things that really matter.'

Sylvia Scarlett, which RKO held back for many months, harmed Kate's reputation again, but her choice of her next three films, all heavy period dramas, almost finished her career entirely. However, the first of the trio, *Mary of Scotland*, had a significant effect on her emotional life.

From the moment Kate saw Maxwell Anderson's play *Mary of Scotland* in New York starring Helen Hayes, she had been convinced she should play Mary Stuart on screen, and wanted Cukor to direct it. But after the disaster of *Sylvia Scarlett*, Berman refused to team them together again. Instead, the producer employed John Ford, a great director, but one totally unsuited to this kind of historical romance. Later,

Kate would say, 'I never cared for Mary. I thought she was a bit of an ass. I would have preferred to do a script on Elizabeth... The script was not very interesting. I never quite understood why Jack Ford was willing to direct it.'

In this heavy-handed but lush production, Kate seems rather remote and uncharacteristically passionless, though there is no lack of regal posturing. Little of Mary Stuart's or Kate's fervour creeps through. Instead the heroine becomes, in Andrew Sarris's words, 'a soft-focused unfairly slandered Madonna of the Scottish moors'.

As in her previous films, Kate insisted on executing most of her own stunts, still trying to prove, as she had done as a child to impress her father, that she could undertake the most difficult physical tasks. In this instance, Mary, wearing high-heeled pumps and a heavy, bulky gown, had to run down a flight of stone steps and then, without pausing, vault on to the back of a lively horse and ride away at breakneck speed side-saddle. Ford demanded a stunt woman do it. 'Mary of Scotland supposedly did it, and I'm a damn good horsewoman,'

Kate replied defiantly. Ford finally gave in, but he sadistically asked her to do the risky scene eleven times before he was satisfied.

Kate's courage delighted Ford, a rugged, hard-drinking, macho Irish Catholic, known to his friends by his real name, Sean. 'You're a hell of a fine girl,' he told her. 'If you'd just learn to shut up and knuckle under, you'd probably make somebody a nice wife.' Married, the father of two children, and twelve years Kate's senior, Ford found himself falling for her. Kate was soon responding to his attentions and began to allow him to dominate her.

After the completion of *Mary of Scotland*, instead of going on his usual week-long binge to Mexico with the boys, Ford followed Kate east to her family home in Fenwick, where they sailed and played golf together. Dr Hepburn considered Ford a philanderer who was taking advantage of his daughter. But Ford was serious enough to speak of divorcing his wife Mary. The fact that they had not been married in the

Victor McLaglen, visiting the set of Mary of Scotland, *chats to Kate and his friend John Ford.*

Roman Catholic Church would make a divorce easier. Yet Mary had once vowed that 'Jack is very religious; he'll never divorce me. I'm going to be Mrs John Ford until I die.'

It is ironic that two of Kate's greatest loves – Spencer Tracy and John Ford – should have been hard-drinking Catholic men, almost as if in rebellion against her father, a Protestant teetotaller. When Kate was a teenager, Dr Hepburn nearly had a fit when he discovered that one of her boyfriends was a Catholic. In his progressive eyes, Catholics were reactionaries, against birth control and votes for women. After her father had greeted the Catholic boy with what she described as 'chill politeness', Kate continued to meet him clandestinely.

When Ford was directing *The Plough and the Stars* at RKO, and Kate was making *A Woman Rebels* at the same studio, in the summer of 1936, they saw each other almost every day and night. Nevertheless, Ford refused to move out of the house he shared with his wife and children. At one stage, however, he did something he had never done before: he went on a bender in the midst of shooting a film. His producer, who found him at home in a drunken coma, phoned Kate (Mary was away), as he felt there was no one else to whom Ford would listen. She rushed to his home and, with considerable difficulty, got him up and drove him to the studio, where she smuggled him into her dressing room and tried to sober him up.

Ford eventually returned to his wife and Kate completed *A Woman Rebels*, about a suffragette of the

1870s, a story she wanted to do to pay homage to her mother's activities. The character, Pamela Thistlewaite, who fights for a woman's right to work, to live alone, to read whatever she pleases and to choose her own husband, suited Kate's personality perfectly. Unhappily, the film, ponderously directed by Mark Sandrich, turned out to be more interested in her relationships with two men (Van Heflin and Herbert Marshall) than in the subject of women's emancipation. Besides, the public were getting bored with this kind of fiery, non-conformist Hepburn heroine.

In *Quality Street*, Kate had the opportunity to play two sides of her screen persona, the self-righteous rebel and the self-conscious outsider. The film, based on a play by James Barrie and set in England during the Napoleonic Wars, tells of Phoebe Throssel, a young woman whose fiancé (Franchot Tone) goes off to war. On his return many years later, he fails to

Left: *Modelling a finely pleated gown of silver lamé, inspired by ancient Greek statuary.*

Right: *One of a range of unusual portraits taken of Kate by Cecil Beaton, the celebrated photographer of the famous.*

recognize Phoebe, who has become a schoolteacher teetering on the brink of spinsterhood. She decides to get her revenge on him by masquerading as her own, non-existent, flirtatious niece.

Quality Street reunited Kate with George Stevens in the hope that they might reproduce the success of *Alice Adams*. However, Stevens had very little sympathy with the subject, and failed to give Kate the direction she needed. 'She became precious, and preciousness was always her weakness,' explained Stevens. 'I should have helped her away from that, and I wasn't strong enough. *Quality Street* was a precious play about precious people, and that infected her.'

Whereas she had been tender and amusing in *Alice Adams*, her overwrought Phoebe Throssel lacked warmth and humour. The *New York Times* claimed that 'such flutterings and jitterings and twitchings, such hand-wringings and mouth-quiverings, such runnings about and eye-brow raisings have not been seen on a screen in many a moon'. Needless to say, *Quality Street* turned out to be another bomb, prompting serious discussions among the RKO brass about Kate's future with the studio.

With another box-office failure to her debit, the news of Leland Hayward's marriage to Margaret Sullavan, and John Ford out of reach, Kate's career and emotional life were at a low ebb. She was particularly susceptible when, to the surprise of many of her friends, she began seeing millionaire industrialist and aviator Howard Hughes on a regular basis.

They had first met during the shooting of *Sylvia Scarlett*. A biplane landed near the film's Malibu location, and out stepped RKO's backer, Howard Hughes. He came over to where Kate and Cukor sat eating during their lunch break and, in his curious high-pitched voice, introduced himself. Kate found him somewhat ridiculous, and displayed her old arrogance. He soon left, but flew back regularly. He then began sending Kate flowers and they saw each other a few times on her return to Hollywood. Gradually, she began to change her opinion of him.

'I don't know what she was doing with Howard Hughes,' commented Anita Loos. 'He had a whole stable of girls, and Kate simply wasn't the type to have anything to do with that kind of thing.' However, Kate was attracted to individualist men of action; she and Hughes shared a passion for aviation, golf and films, and both came from a wealthy background. Although Hughes was as taciturn as she was talkative, he became eloquent when he talked of aeroplanes, and taught Kate to fly.

With nothing planned for her at RKO, Kate announced she would return to the stage in an adaptation of Charlotte Bronte's *Jane Eyre* for the Theatre Guild at $1500 a week, with the hope that John Ford might later film it with her starring. While the play was on tour, Hughes followed in his private plane, attending some performances. In Chicago, he took a suite in the same hotel as Kate, which provoked the headline HUGHES AND HEPBURN TO MARRY.

Getting wind of this romance, John Ford was prompted to declare to Kate that he had decided to leave his wife for her. He then changed his mind again. When *Jane Eyre* was in Baltimore, Kate wrote to Ford to say she had had enough of his vacillations and demanded a final answer. But on her return to LA in May 1937, Ford was still wavering. As a result, Kate moved in with Hughes. On the way to visit her parents, Hughes proposed. She refused. 'Well, I'll never marry,' she recalled thinking at the time, although she had considered marrying Leland Hayward and might have married Ford. Hughes was another matter.

'I want to be a star, and I don't want to make my husband my victim. And I certainly don't want to make my children my victims.'

Speculation on the possible marriage between Kate and Howard Hughes reaches the covers of the movie magazines.

6

'Box-office Poison'

Two of an actress's greatest assets are love and pain. A great actress, even a good actress, must have plenty of both in her life.

On her return to Hollywood in the winter of 1937, Kate, now thirty years old, brooded on the failure of most of her movies to reach a mass audience. It was, therefore, with a great sense of relief that Leland Hayward was able to negotiate a new deal for her at RKO for $75,000 per picture, a miracle considering that she had been blamed for the low box-office returns on her last films.

For the first of the movies under the new contract, Kate suggested George S. Kaufman's *Stage Door*, which had been a huge hit on Broadway in 1936 with Margaret Sullavan. In order to hedge their bets, RKO cast Ginger Rogers in a part equal to Kate's in importance, giving the former higher billing. The two stars proved to be splendid foils for each other, and their barbed exchanges were a delight.

Kate's role was similar to her Oscar-winning characterization in *Morning Glory*, with Adolphe Menjou, also in the earlier film, again playing a Jed Harris-like producer. Like Kate, the character is a society girl who comes to New York determined to make it as an actress; she is well-off, domineering and opinionated; she has a father who disparages her choice of profession and yet gives her financial support; and she receives leading parts before she is capable of playing them. However, unlike the notorious fiasco of *The Lake*, her stage triumph comes in a play called *Enchanted April*, in which she enters clutching a bouquet, repeating the frequently sent-up line, 'The calla lilies are in

Friendly rivals. On the set of **Stage Door** *(1937) chatting to Ginger Rogers, with whom Kate shared top billing.*

Opposite: Kate maturing into a great star despite a series of commercial disasters.

bloom again.' Kate plays the scene beautifully, without a trace of self-mockery.

Gregory La Cava, the director of *Stage Door*, said of Kate, 'She is completely the intellectual actress. She has to understand the why of everything before she can feel. Then, when the meaning has soaked in, emotion comes, and superb work.'

Unlike her last four films, *Stage Door* made a profit. As a test of her popularity it was inconclusive, because it was an ensemble picture, not a star vehicle. But it was significant in that a new Katharine Hepburn emerged, an actress who, after all the melodramas and costume pieces, proved she could play comedy and pathos in modern dress. *Stage Door* also introduced her to Constance Collier, who portrayed a splendid old actress in the picture.

Kate's only slapstick role – in Howard Hawks's Bringing Up Baby *(1938), acting for the second time with Cary Grant.*

Collier became Kate's mentor, drama coach, firm friend and confidante. When Kate began work on her next picture, she felt convinced that the bad times were behind her.

Impressed by her flair for comedy

in *Stage Door*, the studio cast Kate as a dizzy heiress pursuing a stuffy, bespectacled palaeontologist (Cary Grant) in *Bringing Up Baby*. The film's director, Howard Hawks, remarked of Kate, 'She has an amazing body – like a boxer. It's hard for her to make a wrong turn. She's always in perfect balance... This gives her an amazing sense of timing. I've never seen a girl that had that odd rhythm and control.'

Responding to Howard Hawks's rapid-fire direction, both Kate and Grant played at a break-neck speed suitable to the farcical situations, many involving the leopard of the title. Grant, taking his cue from Harold Lloyd, is hilarious, but Kate, though obviously communicating her enjoyment, is far too strident and unvarying for much of the time. A majority of critics now put *Bringing Up Baby* among the best screwball comedies ever made, though it sank in its day.

For her fifteenth motion picture, Kate moved away from RKO for the very first time. George Cukor was to direct *Holiday* at Columbia, and he persuaded studio head Harry Cohn, who had wanted to cast Irene Dunne, to sign Kate in the role she had understudied ten years before. On her first meeting with the infamous Cohn, he

Thought too off the wall for the period, Bringing Up Baby *is now considered the quintessential screwball Thirties comedy.*

observed, 'Leland Hayward tells me you're great in the hay.' Kate went on talking rapidly as if she hadn't heard him. Cohn repeated himself. Kate still did not pause in her conversation, ignoring the remark completely, and Cohn gave up.

The centre of attraction. Kate surrounded by the cast and crew of Holiday. *George Cukor and Cary Grant are on her immediate right.*

Holiday, one of the most stylish of romantic comedies, is about an impecunious noncomformist Johnny Case (Cary Grant) who becomes engaged to the snobby daughter of a millionaire banker, but discovers the girl he really loves is her unconventional sister Linda Seton (Hepburn). Instead of accepting the lucrative bank job offered him, Johnny decides to take a year's holiday with Linda in Europe, both of them giving up a gilded existence. 'Whatever he does is all right with me. If he wants to sit on his tail, he can sit on his tail. If he wants to come back and sell peanuts, Lord how I'll believe in those peanuts!' Kate says with exultant eloquence. As Linda is the archetypal Hepburn heroine – a rebellious society girl endowed with brains and beauty, strong yet unsure of herself – Kate played her with total conviction. The picture also revealed the new, glamorous Katharine Hepburn.

Working away from RKO for the first time, Kate teamed up again with Cary Grant and director George Cukor for Holiday (1938) *at Columbia.*

She had never looked more radiant on screen, with becoming make-up and hairdo, and the most flattering photography. Nevertheless, according to Kate, 'I was so terrible! It was heartbreaking to see how eager, how hard I was trying to impress – too eager. I turned to George [Cukor] and said, "Oh God, why did you hire me?" '

Despite good reviews, Holiday lost money, demonstrating that Depression audiences were unamused by the antics of the idle rich. It was around this time that the Independent Theatre Owners' Association published the names of performers who were, in their terminology, 'box-office poison'. Kate's name headed the list, which included Joan Crawford, Greta Garbo and Marlene Dietrich, all of them stars who portrayed mature, free-spirited women, while ten-year-old Shirley Temple and the teenage Deanna Durbin were the most popular female stars at the box office. Evidently, American cinema audiences in 1938 were looking for an escape into innocence. 'They say I'm a has-been. If I weren't laughing so much I might cry,' Kate commented.

She therefore decided to leave RKO for good, insulted when the studio offered her a role in a B picture called *Mother Carey's Chickens* (a part eventually taken by Ruby Keeler). Kate never worked for the studio again. In May 1938, she left

STAGE
THE MAGAZINE OF
After Dark
MARCH 15, 1939

15¢

Katharine Hepburn
in the
Theatre Guild Production

A lobby card for Holiday, *in which Kate, again as a rich girl, gave one of her most radiant performances.*

'Box-office poison' or not, Kate was still constantly featured on magazine covers like this one from March 1939.

Demonstrating her diving skills, just one of her sporting talents.

An all-round sportswoman, Kate was an excellent tennis player.

Left: *Kate in an uncharacteristic come-on publicity pose in the late 1930s.*

*No longer a false Hollywood
image, but her own woman.*

*The film that relaunched
Kate's career in a big way,
and over which she had
control for the first time.*

Left: *Although not yet seen
in a Technicolor film, Kate
shows herself as a natural
red-haired beauty as she
emerges into superstardom.*

Hollywood for her family home in Connecticut, only to return in triumph.

Swimming and walking occupied most of her time there, and she still took about half a dozen cold showers a day. Looking the picture of health, Kate seemed to flourish away from Hollywood. There was one screen role, however, that she hankered for. Margaret Mitchell's epic novel of the American Civil War *Gone with the Wind* had been published the previous year and Kate had wanted to play Scarlett O'Hara from the time she read the proofs. But to her great disappointment, RKO rejected the book and it was passed on to David O. Selznick. She then pestered Selznick for a chance to play the part. George Cukor was signed to

With thirty-three-year-old Joseph Cotten as Dexter Haven in the hit stage production of Philip Barry's The Philadelphia Story *at the Shubert Theatre in 1939.*

direct the picture and he pressurized the producer to consider Kate. When Selznick finally agreed, she refused a screen test, telling him, 'You know what I look like on the screen. You know I can act. And you know this part was practically written for me. I am Scarlett O'Hara. So what's the matter?'

'Because, my dear, I can't see Rhett Butler chasing you for ten years.'

'Well, David, I may not appeal to you, but some people's idea of sex appeal is different from yours,' she retorted, and stormed out of his office.

Whatever Rhett Butler may have felt, Howard Hughes was still chasing her after two years, and Kate had succeeded in keeping him interested without any commitment on her part. Hughes courted her in high style, flying in and out with expensive gifts – including jewels, although Kate seldom wore jewellery.

In the summer of 1938, Philip Barry brought her a new play of his to read. The character of Tracy Lord in *The Philadelphia Story* bore a great resemblance to Kate, and there is no doubt that Barry had her in mind when he wrote it. She was enthusiastic and, putting up half the money with Hughes, got the Theatre Guild to produce it. Now owner of a quarter of the play, she bought the screen rights from Barry for an additional $25,000. Instead of a guaranteed salary, she took 10 per cent of the gross profits from the New York run and 12 per cent of profits on the road. For the first time in her professional career Kate

Twenty-nine-year-old Van Heflin as Mike Connor in the stage production of The Philadelphia Story. *Heflin was bitter about being passed over in favour of James Stewart for the film version.*

had control over a play, and a possible film, in which she would star.

The Philadelphia Story went straight into rehearsals in the first week of January 1939. Van Heflin, who had appeared with her in *A Woman Rebels*, played Mike, the young newspaperman who falls in love with Tracy, and Joseph Cotten, from Orson Welles's Mercury Theatre, appeared as her ex-husband, C. K. Dexter Haven.

As opening night on Broadway – 28 March 1939 – approached, Kate grew increasingly nervous. She was carrying the label of 'box-office poison' around her neck, Philip Barry had had four flops in six years, and the Theatre Guild had had only one hit in three seasons. Her last appearance on the New York stage had been in the disastrous *The Lake*, six years previously, from which she still bore the scars. But all her fears proved to be unfounded. Both her performance and the play were rapturously received. Even more important to her was that her parents finally accepted that their movie-star daughter had become a fine stage actress.

Kate, Cary Grant and James Stewart were at their sparkling best in The Philadelphia Story *(1940), George Cukor's sophisticated comedy of manners.*

Howard Hughes, weary of pursuing Kate, had turned to a succession of other women, though he remained a close friend and business partner. It was now Van Heflin who could be found most often in her company, and rumours abounded that they were having an affair. But when the run of the play entered its second year, he returned to Hollywood.

Within a few days of opening night, Kate received an offer from MGM for *The Philadelphia Story*. She sold them the rights for $250,000 with a guaranteed approval of director, co-stars and scriptwriter. To nobody's surprise, she chose her friends Cukor to direct and Donald Ogden Stewart to write the screenplay. As neither Joseph Cotten nor Van Heflin was then sufficiently known to movie audiences, she chose Cary Grant and James Stewart to star with her. (Heflin was to feel bitter about this 'betrayal'.) Against Kate's objections, Grant insisted on and received star billing above her.

Few retakes were required on *The Philadelphia Story*, which took eight weeks to shoot, five days under schedule. One of the few additions to the original play was the famous opening scene: a door opens, Grant walks out, Kate appears and heaves a bag of golf clubs after him; he turns around, shoves her in the face and she falls stiffly backwards into the house.

Left: *Katharine Hepburn now given the full, classy, MGM glamour treatment.*

refuses Mike's proposal and remarries Dexter.

In her Adrian frocks, Kate, looking glamorous and self-confident, portrayed Tracy with wit, wisdom and emotional intensity. Cukor said, 'She was perfect as Tracy Lord – she was arrogant but sensitive, she was tough but

George Cukor (behind the sofa) is amused by a rehearsal of The Philadelphia Story *with Kate, James Stewart and Ruth Hussey.*

Loyal as ever to the Theatre Guild, Kate went on tour with the play as soon as the filming finished. When the tour ended – appropriately, in Philadelphia – she gave a touching farewell speech, telling the audience, 'The curtain will never be rung down on this play.'

The plot of the film centres on Tracy Lord, a spoiled Philadelphia society girl about to marry a stuffy man. Ex-husband C.K. Dexter Haven (Cary Grant) arrives on the scene, as do reporters Mike Connor (James Stewart) and Liz Imbrie (Ruth Hussey) of *Spy Magazine* to cover the wedding. Tracy becomes infatuated with Mike, and the duo follow up a drinking session with a moonlight swim, an evening which transforms her from 'ice goddess' to 'real woman'. Earlier she had been told, 'You'll never be a first-class human being till you learn to have some regard for human frailty... but your sense of inner divinity won't allow it.' Now, realizing her deficiencies in her relationship with her ex-husband, whom she really loves, she breaks her engagement,

vulnerable, she didn't care what people thought of her, they had to accept her on her own terms or forget it. Of course, she was far more polished, more skilful than she had ever been before.'

Life magazine wrote, '*The Philadelphia Story* fits the curious talents of the red-headed Miss Hepburn like a coat of quick-dry enamel. It is said to have been written for her. Its shiny surface reflects perfectly from her gaunt, bony face. Its languid action becomes her lean, rangy body. Its brittle smart-talk suits her metallic voice. When Katharine Hepburn sets out to play Katharine Hepburn, she is a sight to behold. Nobody is her equal.'

The picture, which broke all records of the Radio City Music Hall after its première in November 1940, became Kate's professional vindication. She was to begin the new decade with a major triumph behind her, the complete confidence of Louis B. Mayer, a long-term MGM contract and the knowledge that she was part of the most powerful studio in the world.

In 1941, at the time of this MGM publicity still, Kate was gaining more power in the industry, and could make more of her own choices and decisions.

7

Love at Second Sight

*It was a unique feeling that I had for
Spencer Tracy. I would have done
anything for him. My feelings — how
can I describe them? — the door between
us was always open. There were no
reservations of any kind.*

Although they had never met, Katharine Hepburn idolized Spencer Tracy on screen. She admired his skill in not seeming to act at all, his directness and simplicity, his quiet humour and warm personality, his masculine qualities and his rugged yet sensitive features. She had seen most of his pictures, and, above all, cherished his role as Manuel, the Portuguese fisherman, in *Captains Courageous* (1937). 'I can never face the end without weeping so,' she said, after having seen it countless times.

Her heart was set on Spencer Tracy to play C. K. Dexter Haven in the film of *The Philadelphia Story*, certain that he would make a perfect foil for her Tracy Lord, but he had made four pictures in quick succession and needed a rest. Apart from that, he was the kind of man that attracted her most, like her father, not willing to take any guff, proud and strong – stronger than most women. She even mentioned that the name Tracy Lord appealed to her at the time because of her admiration for the actor.

When Kate went to MGM with Ring Lardner Jr's script of *Woman of the Year* in the summer of 1941, she insisted, as she owned the rights, that she would not sell it unless Spencer Tracy co-starred with her. However, Tracy was in Florida on location for *The Yearling* and would not be free for some time. Then the unexpected happened.

For various reasons *The Yearling* was postponed and Tracy was now willing and able to make the film opposite Hepburn. He admired her grace and style in *The Philadelphia Story* and proclaimed her 'a damn fine actress', even suggesting to Louis B. Mayer that she play both female leads in his *Dr Jekyll and Mr Hyde*, an idea Mayer immediately rejected. Nevertheless, Tracy was slightly wary of Kate's reputation for being uppity and her habit of wearing trousers in public. She was in awe of the man she was about to meet, although she had heard tales of the married Tracy's drinking and womanizing.

Kate, at five feet seven, was tall for a Hollywood actress, and with four-inch platform shoes, her hair piled high on her head and her rigid back, she seemed far taller. Tracy was

Opposite: *At her peak, aged thirty-six, two years after meeting Spencer Tracy, the love of her life.*

The beginning of a beautiful friendship. Tracy and Hepburn confront each other for the first time on screen in Woman of the Year *(1942), under the scrutiny of director George Stevens (centre).*

a big man, but not particularly tall at five feet ten and a half inches. On their first meeting, when the film's producer Joseph L. Mankiewicz introduced them, Kate remarked, 'I'm afraid I'm a little tall for you, Mr Tracy.' On seeing Spencer's abashed look, Mankiewicz quipped, 'Don't worry, baby, he'll soon cut you down to size.'

After she left, Tracy turned to Mankiewicz and said, 'Not me, boy, I don't want to get mixed up in anything like that.' Later, when she asked Tracy what he thought of the script, he replied, 'It's all right. Not much to do as it stands – but, Shorty, you better watch yourself in the clinches!' It was the beginning of a beautiful friendship.

From the moment shooting began under George Stevens' direction, something remarkable happened between Hepburn and Tracy. As the camera began to turn, it acted upon them like a magic ray: they fell in love. People around them and those working on the picture started to notice small things. In the first few days Tracy had called Hepburn 'Shorty' or 'that woman', but it gradually became 'Kate' or 'Kath'. She seemed to glow with a new feminine aura, and though she still always wore slacks or jeans, she took more care over her appearance. Stevens recognized the symptoms and backed away from his romantic attachment in a gentlemanly manner.

On the very first day of shooting, Kate's acting was subdued, her usually clear and distinctive diction mumbled. Tracy spoke his lines in an artificial and overstudied manner. 'My God!' cried Mankiewicz. 'They're imitating each other!' Stevens noted, 'From the very beginning of the picture, and their relationship, Spence's reaction to her was a total, pleasant but glacial put-down of her extreme effusiveness. He just didn't get disturbed about doing things immediately; she wanted to do a hundred and one things at once; he was never in a hurry.'

Woman of the Year proved to be

Kate with the characteristic towel wrapped around her head in an off-set moment with Tracy on Woman of the Year.

one of the top earners of the 1941-42 season. *Time* magazine wrote that 'actors Hepburn and Tracy have a fine old time... They take turns playing straight for each other...', and the *Baltimore Sun* recognized that 'his quiet masculine stubbornness and prosaic outlook on life is in striking contrast with her sparkle and brilliance. They make a fine team, and each complements the other.' The writer's comments could just as well have been applied to their real-life romance as well. Most of the nine pictures they did together reflected much of their personal rapport: humorous put-downs, amusing collisions and a mingling of desperation and joy.

Woman of the Year concerned the love-hate marriage of a sophisticated political columnist and a gruff sportswriter, based on Ring Lardner's real-life relationship with Dorothy Parker. The scenario emphasized the feminist angle until, at the rewritten ending, Kate's character submitted to domesticity in order to keep the man she loved. Kate used strong language about the reactionary finale, but it didn't offend Tracy's more conventional view of gender roles. Most of the films they made were really variations on *The Taming of the Shrew*, the message being that a woman who is really a woman must take second place to the man in her life. In all their films together, Kate took second billing. When the writer Garson Kanin once asked, 'Spencer, didn't you ever hear of ladies first?' Tracy replied, 'This is a movie, not a lifeboat.'

It was not long after their first meeting that Kate came brutally into contact with a part of her lover that she would spend the best part of her time fighting. Halfway through shooting of *Woman of the Year*, Tracy disappeared. Friends, and members of the crew who had worked with him before, knew that he had gone on one of his periodic binges. When he was not found at his usual drinking haunts, Kate went from bar to bar searching for him. She finally caught up with him, brought him home, fed him and sobered him up. On the set, for the rest of the

A scene from Woman of the Year, *the first and one of the best of the many Tracy–Hepburn pairings.*

A glamorous 1940 studio portrait presents a vivid contrast to Kate's everyday, more natural look.

picture, she brewed pots and pots of strong tea to serve him. It was all reminiscent of her attempts to keep John Ford off the bottle.

Kate was strongly advised against entering into an affair with Tracy. There were so many good reasons, if there had been a rational option, why it should never have happened. Tracy was only seven years her senior, but already had serious health problems at the age of forty-one. Mainly as a result of excessive drinking, his liver and kidneys had been affected, and his heart was not too strong either. He was often moody, rude and short-tempered, and suffered periods of melancholia.

Another negative aspect was the fact that, as a Catholic, he would never divorce his wife, Louise, though she was Episcopalian. The marriage had eroded, but it had turned into a dependent friendship with strong ties. The Tracys had been married nearly twenty years, through good and bad times. Louise had put aside her own acting career not long after their son of ten months had been diagnosed incurably deaf, dedicating her life to learning how to communicate with him and working for many years to help found and then fund the John Tracy Clinic for Deaf Children. A man of conscience

Sipping fish chowder with her idol President Roosevelt at Mrs Roosevelt's cottage in Hyde Park, New York, in 1940, where a group of artists gathered to give their support for the New Deal.

or character could never walk out on a woman like Louise. How many times had she welcomed him home either drunk or from the arms of another woman – or both – without recrimination?

This had not stopped him having affairs. Kate's friends reckoned that if Tracy had not left his wife for Loretta Young some years previously, he would never set up house with her. She would have to accept the terms of a clandestine relationship with all its pitfalls. But Kate was deeply in love with Tracy, and he saw her as his salvation – a woman who could share his work as well as his life, and accept him for what he was. By loving him, she became a less self-absorbed person and also a better actress.

They seemed an ill-assorted couple, the embodiment of the theory of the attraction of opposites. He was a devout Catholic, she was a free-thinker; he was hard drinking, she was virtually a teetotaller; he was a physical wreck, she was a superb sportswoman; he was of Irish stock born in Milwaukee, Wisconsin, she was the WASP personified born in Hartford, Connecticut; he was a pessimist, she was an optimist; his acting talent lay in doing as little as possible, her style was showy.

On the other hand, they shared the same brand of dry wit and humour, were equally dedicated to their chosen craft and could not tolerate flatterers or sycophants. They both had a no-nonsense attitude to life, did not suffer fools gladly, shunned publicity as much as possible, led extremely private lives and held strong convictions. Both were Democrats and great admirers of Franklin D. Roosevelt; both were repelled by the McCarthy witch-hunts of the 1950s. They loved reading, music and the theatre, were interested in sports, enjoyed discussing politics and had the same intellectual curiosity. They painted together – seascapes, landscapes and scenes through the windows of their hotel bedrooms. They fulfilled each other intellectually, artistically and spiritually. It was a love affair that was sustained and unwavering from 1941 to Tracy's death in 1967 and beyond.

The affection between the co-stars of Woman of the Year *was a genuine one, and this transmitted itself to audiences.*

8

Perfect
Partners

*We balanced each other's natures. We
were perfect representations of the
American male and female.*

Although rumours filtered through, the public at large was never fully aware of Kate and Spencer's affair until the early 1970s. It was Louella Parsons who called it 'the greatest love story never told'. But if Kate and Spencer's real relationship was a clandestine one, they could, at least, relive it in fictional terms for all the world to see. Therefore, they tried to work together as much as possible.

Following the success of *Woman of the Year*, the first Tracy–Hepburn pairing, MGM quickly put them into another vehicle. *Keeper of the Flame* was a competent melodrama, directed by George Cukor, that made the mistake of eliminating any love interest between the couple (the only one of their films to do so). Kate had managed to persuade MGM to make the film because she was fascinated by the character of a resolute woman placed in a tragic position on learning that her dead husband, whom she thought a hero, had been a traitor to his country. Tracy played the investigative reporter who discovers the truth. Because the film pointed to the dangers of creeping fascism in the USA, Kate thought that it would be of valuable assistance to the war effort. But it turned out to have what Cukor called a 'waxwork quality'. Kate herself felt that *Keeper of the Flame* was pretentious and unconvincing. Photographed by William Daniels, Garbo's favourite cameraman, she was made to resemble the Swedish star. 'I didn't like the glamour side of Kate,' Cukor commented. 'I loved the fresh, natural Kate when she forgot to be a movie queen. The subject brought out the movie queen in her, and that wasn't good.'

Not long after Kate and Tracy's return from a trip east, where Kate introduced Spencer to her family, they agreed to make *The Sea of Grass*. Tracy played Colonel James Brewton, a nineteenth-century New Mexico cattle tycoon, obsessed with the grasslands of his family estate, and

A relationship both playful and erotic, it mirrored Tracy and Hepburn's real-life one.

Kate was Lutie Cameron, the strong-willed, sensitive young woman who marries him. Elia Kazan, who had made only one previous feature, was signed to direct. 'I was scared of Kate – I was overpowered by her,' Kazan recalled. 'After all, she was "royalty".' He found her 'a very cool person'. To break down her reserve, Kazan asked her to cry in one scene, and Kate was happy to oblige. However, Louis B. Mayer didn't like the scene. 'The channel of tears is wrong,' he told Kazan. 'They go too near her nostrils.' The director tried to explain that Kate's face was made

The fine horsewoman with Spencer in George Cukor's melodrama Keeper of the Flame *(1942), their second pairing.*

Relaxing while listening to
George Cukor on the set of
Keeper of the Flame.

that way, but Mayer shouted him down. 'Some people cry with their voice, some with their throat, some with their eyes, but she cries with everything, and that is excessive.'

The stilted film reflects the director's inexperience and failure to get more than adequate performances from the two leads. It also suffered from being filmed in a studio, when it cried out for authentic open spaces.

In those early years of the 1940s, Tracy was still battling against the alcoholism which had plagued him during the latter part of the previous decade, and Kate made it her bounden duty to break him of the habit. She conducted a vigorous campaign to separate Tracy from his drinking companions, and succeeded to some degree. He had moved into a modest guest cottage that Cukor had on his grounds and Kate into a hilltop house that had once belonged to silent-screen star John Gilbert.

Kate's routine remained virtually unchanged. She still rose early each morning and was always the first on the set. She always wore the same military student's cap, which she had picked up on a trip to Europe with Luddy in 1932, and an old army fatigue jacket which her brother Richard had left behind on a visit years before. She had a succession of dogs, which she adored, taking them with her on her constant walks around Hollywood. She refused to eat out. 'Whenever I eat out, I pass out – sounds funny, but it's true. I've only been to a restaurant five or six times in my life, and each time I've passed out. My nerves are terrible – if people are watching me, I gobble my food, and then I get sick. So I always eat at home.'

Jack Dawn's oriental make-up for Kate in Dragon Seed *(1944) went some way to help her convince as a Chinese peasant.*

Private as ever, she rarely gave an autograph. On one occasion, some fans begged her. She refused. When one said, 'How dare you refuse? We made you what you are today,' Kate replied, 'Like hell you did!'

In September 1942, Luddy filed for divorce in Hartford under the name of Ogden Ludlow. He claimed desertion and told the court that he doubted the legality of the decree Kate had received in Mexico in 1934. The case appeared on the docket simply as 'Ogden Ludlow v. Katharine H. Ludlow'. Not until the hearing was over did the judge realize the identity of the defendant. A week later, Luddy married a divorced Boston socialite, Elizabeth Albers.

Now at MGM, Pandro Berman, who had once sworn he would never do another film with Kate, came to her with an adaptation of Pearl S. Buck's *Dragon Seed*. The role of the idealistic yet realistic Chinese girl, Jade, appealed to Kate, perhaps because of the challenge of portraying a woman of another culture, but also because the theme was that of the Chinese peasant's long struggle against Japanese aggression.

The $3 million production was filmed largely on location in the San Fernando Valley, where an entire Chinese peasant village was constructed on a 120-acre tract of land. Kate's high cheek-boned features lent themselves well to the Chinese make-up, but her Bostonian voice was less convincing. Yet, despite James Agee's remarks about her 'Peck and Peckish pajamas' and 'her twangy New England Oriental accent', she managed, against all the odds, to create a sympathetic character, even overcoming such risible lines such 'I don't want my baby teethed on Japanese bullets.'

Although she enjoyed making *Dragon Seed*, Kate really wanted to work with Spencer again, as the partnership was good for both of them. With the failure of the dramas *Keeper of the Flame* and *The Sea of Grass*, Kate looked around for a vehicle in which they could return to the lighter bantering mood of *Woman of the Year*. She found it in *Without Love*, the Philip Barry play in which she had starred in a moderately successful fourteen-week limited run in New York towards the end of 1942. On stage, Kate had been the centre of attraction, delivering witty lines while swanning around in her Valentina costumes. With Tracy's considerable presence, the plot gained in substance, becoming a more balanced piece. It is a comedy about a scientist and a rich woman who offers him the basement of her mansion to use as a laboratory. They therefore agree to marry 'without love'.

Towel-headed again, Kate pours herself tea off the set of The Sea of Grass.

Unfortunately, the picture suffered from mediocre direction (Harold S. Bucquet), and a retrograde performance from Kate – full of girlish mannerisms, frequently exclaiming, 'By gum!', grinning and clutching at her throat. She was beginning to be self-conscious about her 'scrawny' neck, which she would cover with scarves and high collars.

With Tracy off the booze and working, Kate took on a couple more parts without him, though neither enhanced her reputation. *Undercurrent*, a reasonably entertaining piece of hokum, directed by Vincente Minnelli, is about a young, rather naive woman who marries a charming and wealthy industrialist (Robert Taylor). Her husband confesses to her that he has a psychopathic brother (Robert Mitchum), who has committed murder and is a constant threat. When the brother finally appears, she becomes convinced that it is her husband who is the killer. Kate was woefully miscast in the role of a defenceless wife, more

Tracy and Hepburn, suspicious of Elia Kazan's 'Method' training, gave the director a hard time on The Sea of Grass.

Above: *A still aptly demonstrating the title of* The Sea of Grass, *though it was actually shot on the MGM back lot.*

Right: *Not one of Tracy and Hepburn's best efforts,* The Sea of Grass *was held back from release by MGM for over a year.*

Overleaf: *Kate in a typically informal pose in slacks and sweater on the set of* Undercurrent *(1946).*

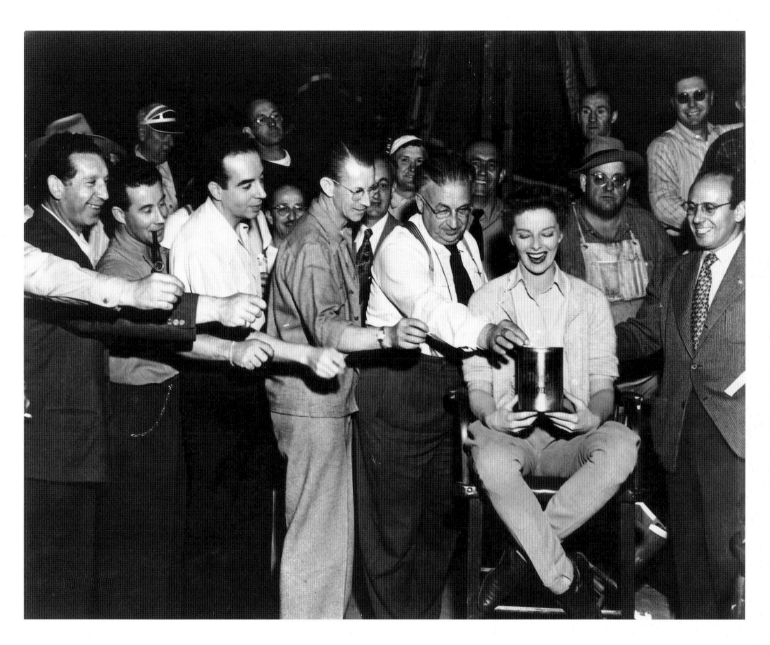

It's a wrap. Kate celebrating with the crew and director Vincente Minnelli (third from left) on the soundstage of Undercurrent.

Smiling again in Without Love *(1945), after two unsuitably dour dramas together.*

suited to the talents of Ingrid Bergman. She mentioned that her greatest difficulty was 'getting the right horrified reaction'.

During the making of *Undercurrent*, Kate became very friendly with Minnelli's wife, Judy Garland. She forced Judy to get up early and take morning walks, and tried, unsuccessfully, to stop her from drinking and taking drugs.

Song of Love was an over-romanticized story based on the marriage of Clara and Robert Schumann. For her role, Kate studied daily with pianist Laura Dubman, a pupil of Artur Rubinstein (who made the recordings for the film), and mastered 'the proper techniques of playing difficult compositions for close-up shooting'.

Artur Rubenstein supplied the music, while Kate displayed pianistic skills in Song of Love.

Rubinstein commented, 'If I hadn't seen it with my own eyes and ears, I wouldn't have believed it! That woman is incredible! She actually does play almost as well as I do! And when she ends and I begin, only I in the whole world could tell the difference!' Actually, Kate was well cast as the determined Clara, who gives up her career to marry the struggling composer (Paul Henreid) and have seven children.

During the war years, Kate was a Roosevelt partisan, but lost faith in the Democratic Party when Truman inherited the office. In 1947, she switched her allegiance to Henry Wallace, who was campaigning for the Presidency on a third party, Progressive, ticket. He was labelled 'a Communist dupe'. In May 1947, when Wallace was barred from using the Hollywood Bowl for a political

For her role as piano virtuoso Clara Schumann in Song of Love *(1947), Kate took lessons from Laura Dubman, former pupil of Artur Rubenstein.*

The Tracy–Hepburn union was in good fettle during the shooting of Frank Capra's political comedy–drama State of the Union *(1948).*

address, Kate agreed to participate in an anti-censorship rally held in Los Angeles. In her speech, she attacked the House UnAmerican Activities Committee. 'The artist since the beginning of time has always expressed the aspirations and dreams of his people. Silence the artist and you have silenced the most articulate voice the people have.'

Poles apart politically off screen, Kate and Adolphe Menjou had to put enmity aside while working together on State of the Union.

Kate's speech was impressive and carefully prepared, but she was negligent about her clothes. 'At first I was going to wear white,' she recalled. 'And then I decided they'd think I was the dove of peace, so I

wore pink. Pink! How could I have been so dumb?' Although her name came up at the HUAC, she was never called before it. In 1947, she joined a group of actors and directors, led by John Huston and William Wyler, who formed the Committee for the First Amendment, a group dedicated to combating 'the unfavorable picture of the film industry arising from testimony before the House Committee on UnAmerican Activities'. Like France during the Dreyfus case, Hollywood was divided into two enemy camps. This became apparent while Kate was shooting her next film.

It was time for her to have another success. It

came with Tracy again in *State of the Union*, directed by Frank Capra. Claudette Colbert was originally cast as the estranged wife of a presidential candidate, but when she refused to work beyond 5 p.m., the director sacked her. Capra phoned Tracy to tell him the bad news. Tracy, of course, knew someone who could fill the role. 'The bag of bones has been helping me rehearse. Kinda stops you, Frank, the way she reads the woman's part... She might do it for the hell of it.'

By Monday morning, Kate was on the set ready to start shooting. There was, however, a touchy problem. Adolphe Menjou, who played the crafty campaign manager, had co-operated with the HUAC, while Kate had spoken out against the committee's 'smear campaign'. Capra ordered the soundstage closed as she and Menjou performed their scenes, because the press were anxious to report any friction between them on the set. As professionals, they refused to let their personal rancour show, but it was a sad contrast to their pleasant working rapport years before in *Morning Glory* and *Stage Door*.

Tracy portrays a liberal Republican seeking the Presidency, and living apart from his wife. In order to show the electorate that he is a solid citizen, she is asked to return and masquerade as his loving spouse. But she watches her husband alter his values and decides to speak up, pointing out that the people with whom he has chosen to throw in his lot are greedy, grasping and corrupt. He listens to her and understands what he has done. On the radio, he announces he is taking his name off the nominating slate because he feels he is not worthy of consideration on the voters' part.

Of Tracy and Hepburn, Capra commented that when they 'played a scene, cameras, lights, microphones, and written scripts ceased to exist. And the director did just what the crews and other actors did – sat, watched, and marveled.' Though Kate played the non-flashy part with a nice balance of humour and conviction, *Time* magazine thought that 'Hepburn's affectation of talking like a woman simultaneously trying to steady a loose dental brace sharply limits her range of expression.' *State of the Union*, though taking itself a little too seriously, cemented Tracy and Hepburn as a team in the public eye.

During the halcyon days between 1942 and 1949, when they were paired six times, Kate and Spencer continued to live in separate homes. Kate ran both households in her capacity as Tracy's companion, secretary, nurse, cook and chauffeur. She even managed to stop his drinking. On weekends when they were not working she kept him as occupied as she could. They walked, swam, talked and painted. Everything in her life, including her choice of film roles, was dictated by Tracy's needs. On pictures in which she did not appear with him, she would still drive him to the studio, remain with him on the set, drive him home and cook him a meal.

In 1948, taking the opportunity to spend a stretch of time in England with Kate, Tracy accepted the lead in *Edward My Son*. During the shooting, he was a guest of Laurence Olivier and Vivien Leigh at their huge thirteenth-century mansion, Notley Abbey, while Kate had a suite at Claridge's. He could not stay with her at the hotel, and they would not have felt at ease together at Notley. It was one of the coldest English winters for decades, and Spencer shivered in the cavernous rooms of the abbey. As a result he and Kate were glad to be able to film *Adam's Rib* in New York in the spring, under George Cukor's direction. During the amiable atmosphere of shooting, Kate was able to live in her house on East 49th Street, while Spencer stayed at the Waldorf Towers.

Adam's Rib (the original title *Man and Wife* was vetoed by the MGM front office as being indiscreet) was written by Garson Kanin and his wife Ruth Gordon with Tracy and Hepburn in mind. It concerned a pair of lawyers, husband and wife, who find themselves on opposite sides in a court case. The

Cole Porter (at the piano) composed the lovely song 'Farewell, Amanda' especially for Adam's Rib, *in which it is sung to Kate.*

film, heralded by the billboards as 'The Hilarious Answer to Who Wears the Pants!!', helped give MGM a financial shot in the arm. The *New York Times* wrote that Tracy and Hepburn's 'perfect compatibility in comic capers is delightful to see. A line thrown away, a lifted eyebrow, a smile or a sharp, resounding slap on a tender part of the anatomy is as natural as breathing to them. Plainly, they took pleasure in playing this rambunctious spoof.'

At the end of the picture, Kate delivers a speech which could well have been made by her mother. 'An unwritten law stands back of a man who fights to defend his home. Apply the same to this maltreated mother. We ask no more. Equality! Deep in the interior of South America, there thrives a civilization, older than ours... In this vast tribe, members of the female sex rule and govern and systematically deny equal rights to the men – made weak and puny by years of subservience. Too weak to revolt. And yet how long have we lived in the shadow of like injustice?'

Adam's Rib, probably their most sparkling picture as a team, had them doing what they did best together, sparring affectionately and wittily in a bouncy battle of the sexes. The tailor-made dialogue by the Kanins, who knew Kate and Spencer very well, suited the stars' personalities admirably and underscored both their on- and their off-screen relationship. A home-movie sequence was very much modelled on how the couple behaved 'at home'.

For some months following *Adam's Rib* they looked for another script that would be right for both of them. When nothing suitable materialized, Tracy went into *Malaya*, an uninspiring action melodrama. Kate, meanwhile, was delighted to be able to take up an offer to play Rosalind in a Broadway production of *As You Like It*, as she had never tackled Shakespeare

*Turning on the waterworks –
an effective weapon in the
battle of the sexes waged in
George Cukor's delightful
comedy* Adam's Rib *(1949).*

before. 'I realize I'm putting my head
on the line,' she said. 'But for me, the
personal satisfaction justifies the
risk.'

She brought Michael Benthall
from England to direct, and her dear
friend Constance Collier to coach
her in the role, working with the older actress for
three hours a day for eight months.

Proud of working on a project she considered

worthwhile, Kate invited her mother to accompany
her to a few of the cities on tour. Mrs Hepburn
agreed, and Kate played to her mother as much as she
did to her audiences. However, she knew she was
taking a risk in leaving Tracy, who
was finding it increasingly difficult to
cope without her during a nine-week
pre-New York tour and then a
longish run. While she was away, he
started drinking again and phoned

*Kate listening intently to her
screen mentor George Cukor
on the set of* Adam's Rib,
*considered the best of the
team's comedies.*

'From the east to western Inde, No jewel is like Rosalind.' Kate in As You Like It at the Cort Theatre, New York, in 1950.

her about three times a day.

As soon as *Malaya* was completed, Tracy caught up with Kate in Cleveland, where he promised to give up alcohol. But during *As You Like It*'s 145 performances on Broadway, Spencer was seen reeling into and out of Kate's apartment night after night. None of the cast ever saw Spencer, who was smuggled in and out of tour hotels in the freight elevator, because he and Kate were determined to keep their loving relationship a secret from almost everyone.

In March 1951, Kate came home to West Hartford. The tour with *As You Like It* had left her physically exhausted but feeling more at ease about her future. Life in Hartford, despite the fact that her brothers and sisters were all married and living away, had not changed. At seventy-five, her father still went to his office on weekdays. Her mother's devotion to birth control and women's rights had not wavered.

On 17 March Kate and Dr Hepburn came in from a brisk walk a few minutes late for afternoon tea. They found the table set, the teapot filled with hot, freshly brewed tea, and the house unnaturally quiet. Exchanging frightened glances, they ran upstairs without a word. Mrs Hepburn had recently had a small heart infarction, and they were not wrong in suspecting what they would find. Kit Houghton Hepburn, at seventy-three, was dead, lying gracefully across her bed. Kate had adored her, and it was painful to realize that this brilliant woman was gone.

'The thing about life is that you must survive,' Kate later said. 'Life is going to be difficult and dreadful things will happen. What you do is to move along, get on with it and be tough. Not in the sense of being mean to others, but tough with yourself and making a deadly effort not to be defeated.'

9

An Unmarried Woman

I never was a child and I never was a mother. I was an Aunt Kat. Sometimes the oldest in a big family turns out that way. I helped raise the others.

Spencer Tracy still considered it a matter of principle that he and Kate lived apart, although both of his children were grown and his son John, despite his deafness, had married. Kate was eager to find a script that would enable her to return to Hollywood, but suitable ones were hard to come by. At forty-four, she realized there were few screenplays that centred on women entering or in middle age, whereas such roles for men were bountiful. She finally found what she was looking for in *The African Queen*, opposite Humphrey Bogart and directed by John Huston, although it meant going all the way to the Belgian Congo to make it.

The African Queen was the name of the rusty old river steamer which took scruffy, profane, unshaven, gin-drinking captain Charlie Allnut (Bogart, winning his only Oscar) and prim, scrawny, Bible-quoting spinster missionary Rose Sayer (Hepburn) down the Congo River during World War I. On the trip, during which they negotiate rapids, shallows and storms, finally succeeding in blowing up a German gunboat, the ill-matched pair learn from each other and fall in love.

At first Kate behaved towards Bogart with a certain disdain, as if out of habit, until he shook her and said, 'You ugly, skinny old bag of bones! Why don't you come down to earth?' Kate, staring him right in the eye, replied, 'Down where you're crawling? All right!' She laughed, everyone laughed, and from that moment, she and Bogart (and Lauren Bacall, who had come along for the ride) became close friends.

Gracefully entering early middle age and a new phase in her career in 1952.

'Bogie hated Africa, but for me it was a glorious adventure,' Kate wrote. It was also a hazardous one. There was a moment when Kate had to go into the water to release the boat, which was stuck in the reeds. 'Oh!' she said, when Huston asked her to do this. 'The river's full of crocodiles!'

'Don't worry. I'll have my prop men fire a few rounds of ammunition into the water. You'll find the

crocodiles get scared by the noise, and they'll vanish,' Huston assured her.

'Yes, but what about the deaf ones?' Kate retorted. She went in anyway.

Ironically, because of her temperance, she got dysentery. 'I was so busy complaining about Bogie and John drinking hard liquor I tried to shame them by drinking water in their presence at mealtimes. Well, the water was full of germs! They never got sick, and I had the Mexican trots, and was in bed every day for weeks! I thought I was going to die – and in the Belgian Congo!'

The hard drinker and the tee-totaller, the sinner and the missionary. The inspired pairing of Bogie and Kate in John Huston's The African Queen *(1951).*

She found Huston brilliant in flashes, as when he told her to base her character of Rose Sayer on Eleanor Roosevelt when she visited the hospitals of the wounded soldiers, always with a smile on her face. 'He had felt that I was playing Rosie too seriously, and that since my mouth turned down anyway it was making the scenes heavy. Since I (as Rosie) was the sister of a minister, my approach to everyone and everything had to be full of hope... In short, he told me exactly how to play the part.'

Wearing little if any make-up to cover her abundant freckles, and exposing her scraggy neck, her gaunt face smudged with mud, Kate bravely abandoned all semblance of glamour, presenting herself exactly as she was. The box-office triumph of this first Technicolor feature for Huston, Bogart and Hepburn could be attributed to its skilful blending of comedy, drama and thrills, its authentic exotic setting, and the inspired pairing of Hepburn and Bogart, the missionary and the sinner, between whom an unlikely romance begins to blossom. They both gave among their most appealing performances, and the film carried the stars to new success in what were essentially character parts.

While in Africa, Kate wrote daily letters to Tracy; these were taken back to the village once a week by native runners, and then picked up by launch, finally reaching Léopoldville, where there was a post office. John Huston relates in his autobiography, 'I remember the many nights I sat with Kate on the top deck of the paddle boat and watched the eyes of the hippos in the water all around us... We talked about nothing and everything. But there was never any idea of romance – Spencer Tracy was the only man in Kate's life.'

But if Tracy was the man in her life, she was the

life in her man. Depressed by Kate's absence, he began drinking heavily again. After location shooting on *The African Queen* was completed on 17 July 1951, Hepburn and Bogart had to spend an extra six weeks filming in England. Tracy had arrived in London earlier to await her. There he met Joan Fontaine at a dinner party and later phoned the actress to ask her out. Fontaine declined the invitation out of respect for Kate, and also reminded Tracy that he was a married man. 'I can get a divorce whenever I want to,' he told her. 'But my wife and Kate like things just as they are.'

Back in America, Kate rolled up her sleeves and got to work on Tracy again, brewing endless cups of coffee, insisting he take cold showers, go for walks and swim every day. Now completely grey, Spencer looked much older than his fifty-one years, but Kate got him into reasonable shape again. She was greatly helped in her efforts by the fact that their good friends Garson Kanin and Ruth Gordon had another made-to-order script ready for the two of them.

Husband-and-wife writers Garson Kanin and Ruth Gordon discuss their screenplay of Pat and Mike *with the friends for whom they wrote it. It was a happy experience for both stars.*

Pat and Mike was a happy experience for both stars and for audiences everywhere. Filmed almost entirely at the Riviera Country Club in Pacific Palisades, it concerned the loving and bantering relationship between a sports promoter and an all-round sportswoman. A favourite line has Tracy saying in a broad Brooklyn accent, when he first claps eyes on Kate, 'Not much meat on her, but what there is, is cherce [choice].'

Looking ten years younger than she had in *The African Queen*, Kate got a rare chance to show off her legs in a short white tennis skirt. She plays a professional golfer and tennis player, but whenever her sexist fiancé is around she feels inferior and her game deteriorates. By the end of the picture, she has dumped him and married sports promoter Tracy, although she has to prove she's weaker than him in order to protect his male ego. *Pat and Mike* is another example in a 1950s Hollywood movie of struggling feminism, manacled in the end by patriarchal ideology.

With her MGM contract at an end (Tracy remained with the studio for three more years until his erratic behaviour got him fired), Kate became obsessed with playing the role of Epifania, Shaw's outrageously spoiled madcap heiress in *The Millionairess*, on stage. 'I adored the play. Everyone kept saying, "Why do you want to do it? It's such a bad play." Well, I thought it was fun, and I still do. It portrays a wonderful character. My mother worshipped Shaw. She knew everything he'd ever written. Backwards. So did my

A rare glimpse of Kate's shapely legs during a practice game for her role as a tennis champ in Pat and Mike *(1952).*

father. A great deal of Shaw was read out loud at home. He was sort of a god.'

Epifania, one of Shaw's 'superwomen', is a role that provides ample scope for an intelligent and vibrant actress. The London opening of *The*

Millionairess at the New Theatre in June 1952 was a triumph, being ecstatically received by Kenneth Tynan in the *Observer*, while another newspaper was headlined 'HEPBURN PLAYS SHAW – AND WINS'. Michael Benthall, who had directed Kate in

Robert Helpmann as the Egyptian doctor and Kate as Epifania in Michael Benthall's production of George Bernard Shaw's The Millionairess *at the Shubert Theater, New York, in October 1952.*

As *You Like It*, disguised the play's weaknesses by mounting a glamorous production, with the star dressed in Pierre Balmain gowns, one of which was an eye-catching jewel-encrusted organdie ball gown.

Kate was joined by Tracy, who flew in to be with her during much of the limited season of twelve weeks in London. When *The Millionairess* reached New York, it was greeted coldly, many of the reviewers accusing Kate of storming, fuming and carrying on excessively in a role that inclined to highlight the more strident side of her personality. Despite this, Kate tried to get the play made into a film, in which she would co-star with Alec Guinness; the director was to be Preston

Sturges, who was in very poor physical shape at the time and drinking heavily. When finances were not forthcoming for the project, Kate decided to give up work for a couple of years in order to keep an eye on Spencer, while he made a number of movies.

Once Kate was confident that her loved one could be left alone again, she took up the tempting offer to make *Summertime*, for David Lean in Venice. There she stayed in a splendidly furnished apartment on the Grand Canal, with a beautiful garden on the river, a cook, butler and maid, and a private gondola. But her absence again created a deep void for Tracy.

He was set to make *Tribute to a Bad Man* opposite Grace Kelly. Rumours reached Kate in Italy of a romance between Tracy and the cool, blonde beauty. When reproached by Kate, Spencer flew over to visit her in Venice for a short period to reassure her that his dinner dates with the future Princess Grace of Monaco had been strictly business.

Summertime concerns a brief encounter between a married antique dealer (Rossano Brazzi) and an unmarried midwestern schoolteacher (Hepburn). The suave Latin lover tells her, 'You Americans think too much about sex instead of doing something about it,' just before she succumbs to his kiss. The romance ends when she breaks it off on moral grounds. Having had her illicit cake, she leaves Venice clutching her crumbs of comfort. As Jane Hudson, Kate overdoes her scrawny, tearful spinster bit, coming to Venice eager to take in all the sights, and hoping to find a 'magic explosion', an expression hardly applicable to the finished film, given David Lean's tame direction. Upstaging everyone was La Serenissima, the city of Venice, well-photographed in Technicolor by Jack Hildyard, which contributed to the film's great success.

The technical difficulties of filming in Venice were endless; even Kate found it exhausting, not having entirely recovered from the dysentery she had contracted in Africa. All the equipment had to be floated on launches or barges, and noisy crowds often ruined key scenes. The most difficult sequence in the picture, and the most famous, was the one in which Kate, photographing an antique shop, backs too

The famous scene in David Lean's Summertime *(1955) in which Kate falls into a filthy Venice canal, watched by little Gaitano Audiero. Her eyes never fully recovered from the infection she picked up.*

close to the edge of a canal and falls into it. It took four takes.

'I knew how dirty the water was, so I took all kinds of precautions – even washed my mouth with antiseptic, put special dressing on my hair, wore shoes that wouldn't waterlog. But like an idiot I forgot my eyes. When I fell in, I had a startled look, with my eyes open... Well, the water was a sewer! Filthy, brackish, full of trash! When I got out, my eyes were running. They've been running ever since. I have the most ghastly infection – I'll never lose it till the day I die. When people ask me why I cry a lot in pictures, I say, mysteriously, "Canal in Venice." '

Uncomfortable in the muggy heat that settled on Venice in that summer of 1954, sometimes weak and ill, upset by her distance from Tracy and irritated by the slowness of the crew, Kate made herself unpopular. After Tracy's departure, she complained, 'Nobody asked me to dinner. They went off and left me alone. I felt rather angry about that. I wandered off by myself through Venice feeling very lonely and neglected, and sat down by the canal and looked in the water, and while I was sitting like that, a man came over to me and said, "May I come and talk to you?" Only it wasn't Rossano Brazzi. It was a French plumber... It was my own fault entirely. I have brought it upon myself. I am rather a sharp person. I have a sharp face and a sharp voice. When I speak on the telephone, I snap into it. It puts people off, I suppose.'

On her return from Venice, Kate found it impossible to resist the offer of a tour of Australia in three Shakespeare plays, *The Taming of the Shrew*, *Measure for Measure* and *The Merchant of Venice*, playing opposite her friend Robert Helpmann, who had co-starred with her in *The Millionairess*. Tracy took her acceptance of the tour as a personal affront. On the day she left for Australia in May 1955 he began to drink heavily. Shooting on *Tribute to a Bad Man* was due to start on 1 June. Tracy arrived at the Colorado desert location six days late, without any

explanation to director Robert Wise. Two days later he disappeared again, causing panic among the crew. Calls were placed to Kate in Australia. Soon after, Tracy was fired and his twenty-one-year MGM contract terminated. Thereafter, he spent much of his time drowning his sorrows and calling Kate, a situation not calculated to help her concentration during her demanding Australian tour. She determined on her return never again to leave him for any length of time. She also took the rumours about Tracy and other women seriously enough to make sure he didn't stray.

The gossip that Tracy would never be hired again in Hollywood was silenced when he was nominated for an Oscar in 1955 for *Bad Day at Black Rock*. (Kate was nominated in the same year for *Summertime*.) But he was a very sick man from then onwards. His liver had deteriorated, his heart and lungs were weak. Kate cut down her own smoking drastically in an effort to help him stop, and she made sure he ate healthily, took exercise and lost weight. She nursed him, cheered him up and encouraged him to keep working. When Paramount signed him to do *The Mountain*, she accompanied him to Chamonix in France for the location shooting. It was not the best choice of subject for Tracy, not only because he was unconvincing as a Swiss shepherd, but also because the high altitude and the climbing gave him breathing difficulties and put a strain on his heart and lungs. Kate managed to remain discreetly in the background during filming, but hardly left his side when the day's work was done.

With *The Mountain* being completed at Paramount in Hollywood, Kate accepted *The Rainmaker*, opposite Burt Lancaster, at the same time and at the same studio so they could be together as much as possible. The story concerns a tense twenty-seven-year-old spinster Lizzie Curry (forty-something Hepburn), who cares for her father and two brothers on a south-western farm plagued by drought. A charming conman, Starbuck (Lancaster), arrives,

Kate and co-star Burt Lancaster confer on the set of The Rainmaker *(1956), though their relationship was relatively cool.*

other, and each resented the other's power over Kate.

In January 1956, Kate flew to London to film a *Ninotchka*-type comedy, *The Iron Petticoat*, at Pinewood Studios with Bob Hope. Hope arrived with an entourage of gag writers who immediately began rewriting the script, weighting the film in his favour. Despite her great care in learning a Russian accent for the role of the stiff Soviet airwoman who falls for the frivolities of capitalism (such as Balmain dresses), Kate was plainly ill at ease playing Bob Hope's stooge.

In the spring, Spencer and Kate flew to Cuba where he was to start filming *The Old Man and the Sea* under Fred Zinnemann's direction. Leland Hayward, Kate's ex-agent and ex-lover, now a producer, had persuaded Tracy that he was the only man to play the ancient Mexican fisherman of Ernest

giving Lizzie more self-confidence and claiming he can bring rain.

Kate made a brave attempt to play a rough, awkward, uneducated farm woman, but, although some genuine passion and humour emerged, it remained a deft, rather theatrical performance from too mature, too knowing an actress. Anyway, it was her third plain spinster act in a row, and it was beginning to pall.

The Rainmaker was finished shortly before Christmas 1955, and Tracy accompanied Kate to Fenwick for the holidays. Some competitiveness existed between him and Dr Hepburn. In fact, the two men were too similar in many ways to like each

Hemingway's novella. Unhappy about the film, Tracy began to tour the Havana bars, after which Kate would get him back to the rambling, fourteen-room villa where they were staying. Between watching Tracy on set and off, Kate managed to find time to paint a number of colourful Cuban seascapes.

The shooting proved arduous for Tracy, who was forced to play many scenes in an open boat, sometimes in difficult weather conditions, with Zinnemann driving him on relentlessly. After watching some of the rushes, Hayward and Hemingway, with some prodding from Kate, had Zinnemann fired, and the whole project was postponed. (It was later shot in a tank in Hollywood

Playing straight woman to

Bob Hope in The Iron

Petticoat *(1956) was not to*

Kate's liking.

by John Sturges.) On their return to California, Kate was determined that Spencer would never again have to endure any gruelling location work.

Happily, they were soon given an opportunity to make their first film together since *Pat and Mike* five years earlier. At first Tracy was against making *The Desk Set*, but he didn't want to deprive Kate of the pleasure of doing another film with him. Kate played an extremely intelligent woman in charge of a library who can answer the most abstruse questions immediately. She and her staff are convinced they will be made redundant when Tracy installs a computer in their office.

Although enjoyable, the picture, directed by Walter Lang, lacked the oomph of Hepburn and Tracy's previous confrontations, being a rather more leisurely affair. But, supremely at ease with each other, they demonstrated they had lost nothing of their comic timing.

Working in Hollywood again, going for long walks, painting, reading and listening to music in Kate's company gave Tracy a new lease of life. They were closer to each other than ever, but Kate was still an actress who needed to stretch herself.

Happily on screen again

together after five years, in

The Desk Set *(1957).*

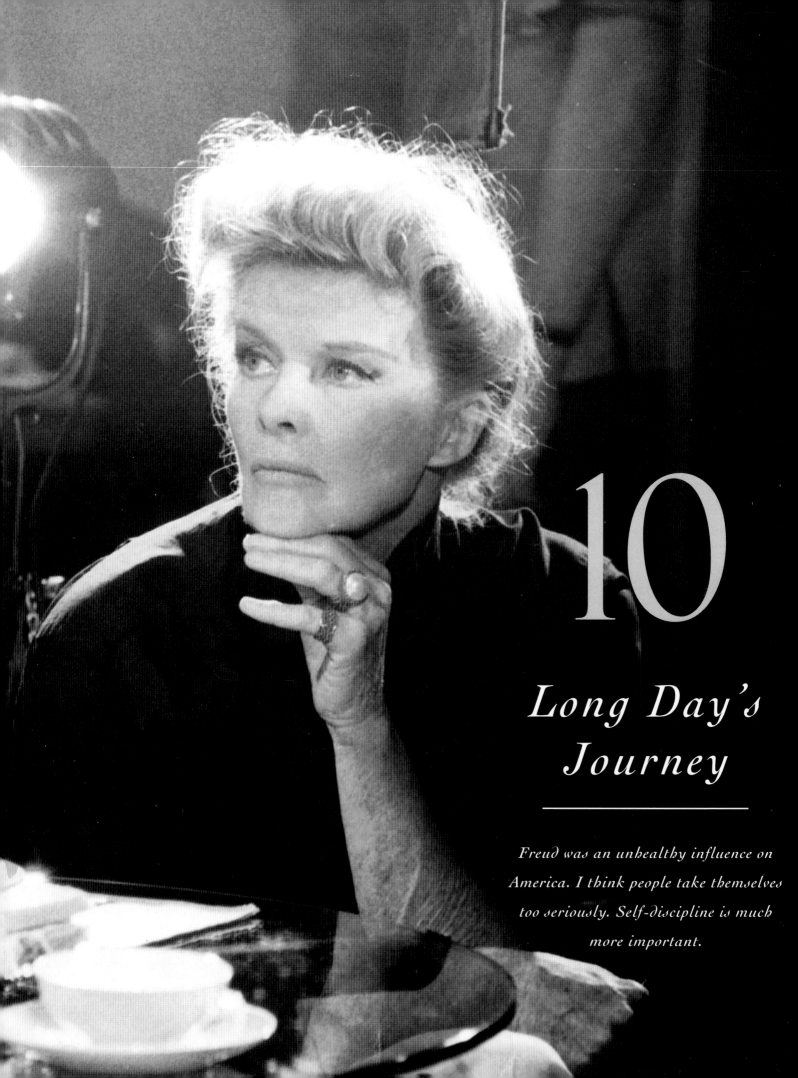

10

Long Day's Journey

*Freud was an unhealthy influence on
America. I think people take themselves
too seriously. Self-discipline is much
more important.*

The year 1957 began with the news that Humphrey Bogart was terminally ill with cancer. On 13 January 1957, Spencer and Kate paid their last visit to him. Emaciated and in great pain, Bogie still managed to smile and joke. After half an hour by his bedside, Kate stood up and leaned over and kissed him. Tracy took his hand. 'Goodbye, Spence. Goodbye, Kate,' Bogart said, instead of 'Goodnight.' When they were leaving, Tracy turned to Kate and said, 'Bogie's going to die.' In fact, he lapsed into a coma the next day, and was dead twenty-four hours later.

Although Kate was now fifty, at the peak of her powers, no films she wanted to do came her way. Consequently she decided to appear in two productions for the American Shakespeare Theatre in Stratford, Connecticut, in the summer of 1957, as Portia in *The Merchant of Venice* and as Beatrice in *Much Ado About Nothing*. John Houseman, the artistic director of the festival, recalled, in his book *Final Dress*, how Kate kept talking about Tracy 'with a mingling of loyalty, tenderness and admiration' during the whole season. She also spoke continually of his imminent arrival from Los Angeles to see her. 'Finally,' Houseman writes, 'the great day came when Kate, with a young girl's enthusiasm, proclaimed that this time Spencer was really coming. His plane ticket was bought and all arrangements were made. On the evening of his arrival... she drove off alone, in a state of high excitement, that she made no attempt to conceal, to Idlewild, to meet him. Soon after she had left, there was a phone call from California. Somehow, on the way to Burbank, Spencer had got lost and missed his plane. He never did appear.'

Kate got mixed reviews for her Shakespearian heroines, but, as always, many in the audience came just to see the movie star. During one performance, someone stood up and took a flash photograph. Kate stopped centre stage and faced the audience.

Kate, entering her sixtieth year, waits patiently for a shot to be set up on Guess Who's Coming to Dinner? *(1967).*

'There will be no more of that or we won't go on,' she said in a stentorian voice, before returning to her scene. When criticized for interrupting the flow of the play, Kate replied with a laugh, 'Well, I guess I would have been a great school principal.'

After the Shakespeare tour, Kate continued to keep fit by jogging and playing tennis wherever she was. She read assiduously and painted her seascapes of both coasts. Her experiences with the flora and fauna in Africa and Australia had

Between rehearsals for The Merchant of Venice, *in which she played Portia, at the American Shakespeare Festival in Stratford, Connecticut, in July 1957.*

enhanced her feeling for nature. She had begun to understand herself more, and had come to terms with her faults. 'Stone-cold sober, I found myself absolutely fascinating,' she said years later.

Aware that Tracy would need constant attention, Kate began to think seriously in 1957 and 1958 of retiring from the screen for good. For eighteen months, she spent most of her time caring for him. Uppermost

Watched by Montgomery Clift and Joseph L. Mankiewicz, Kate manages a laugh on the set of Suddenly Last Summer *(1960), although she hated making the film.*

in her mind was finding suitable scripts worthy of his great talent. She looked no further than *The Last Hurrah*, directed by John Ford. Kate was especially watchful on the set at Columbia, as the supporting cast was made up almost exclusively of members of his old Wednesday night drinking circle. She needn't have worried, as by now they had all reformed.

There was, however, a slight uneasiness on the set, because both Ford and Kate still retained a deep affection for each other. According to Barbara Leaming's highly speculative biography of Hepburn,

As the monstrous Mrs Venable, facing the wrath of her daughter-in-law Elizabeth Taylor in Suddenly Last Summer, *passively observed by Montgomery Clift.*

'Kate seemed frightened of his feelings, and of her own. He loved that in private she still addressed him as Sean. He cherished her visits to his office... He leapt on every reference to their shared past... she remembered all that had passed between them.'

A short while later, Kate decided to make another film, reuniting herself with two old and valued associates, producer Sam Spiegel and director Joseph L. Mankiewicz, for a version of Tennessee Williams' one-act play *Suddenly Last Summer*, adapted by Gore Vidal. She was asked to play the role of Mrs Venable, a monstrous, bloodsucking caricature of an American mother,

whose homosexual son, Sebastian, has been 'cannibalized' by youths. In order to conceal the secret, she has Sebastian's cousin Catherine (top-billed Elizabeth Taylor), who witnessed the assault and murder, committed to a sanitarium and insists on the girl's having a lobotomy to destroy her memory.

This often ludicrous Gothic melodrama was unlike anything Kate had done hitherto, and she thoroughly disliked the character she was playing. On top of which, for reasons of economy, the film was shot in England, and Spencer was in Hollywood suffering from emphysema. As always, her separation from him was unsettling. In addition, she spent her time duelling with Mankiewicz over the interpretation of the matriarch and what she felt was the director's cruel behaviour towards an ailing and

Opposite: *A contemplative portrait taken in London in 1959 at the time of* Suddenly Last Summer.

Left: *Kate joking around by rolling up the leg of her celebrated slacks during the making of* Suddenly Last Summer.

'Age cannot wither her.' In Antony and Cleopatra *with Robert Ryan at Stratford, Connecticut, in July 1960.*

both she and Elizabeth Taylor were nominated for Best Actress Oscars.

Kate was vastly relieved to return to America and her beloved Spencer. Apart from two months playing Cleopatra and Viola at the Shakespeare Festival in Connecticut in the summer of 1960, Kate seldom left his side. It was around that period that stories began to appear in print implying that Tracy and Hepburn were romantically involved, but little else was revealed. Insinuations were generally ignored, people preferring to see them as good companions of long standing. Until 1962, Tracy and his wife were still being photographed together. The deification of Mrs Spencer Tracy and her husband, nicknamed 'The Pope' by David Niven, prevented public gossip and censure.

distressed Montgomery Clift, who was existing on a diet of codeine tablets washed down with brandy. It was also the first time in her career that she was supporting another woman star.

Mankiewicz recalled that 'on the last day of shooting, Kate came up to me, looked me in the eye, and spat. On the floor. Then she went into Sam Spiegel's office and spat on his floor. She never worked with either of us again.' Another witness, the actor Gary Raymond, remembered her spitting in the director's face. Kate claimed never to have seen the film, and never discussed it, though

In 1960 producer-director Stanley Kramer, who worshipped Tracy, offered him the meaty role of the defence lawyer in the notorious 1925 'monkey' trial in *Inherit the Wind.* Kate sat in the corner of the set knitting and peering over the rims of her spectacles from time to time to watch a scene. She was as protective of him as ever. So splendid was Tracy in the role that Kramer implored him to take the part of the American judge in *Judgment at Nuremberg,* to be filmed in the city of the title in 1961.

Because of his admiration for

Kate applying her make-up in preparation for her role as Mary Tyrone in Long Day's Journey into Night *(1962), directed by Sidney Lumet.*

Kramer, Tracy agreed, although he hated travelling. But at the airport, as Kate and he were ready to leave, he suddenly had second thoughts. He hadn't been well for some weeks and wondered whether he could withstand the flight (he had difficulty breathing at high altitudes) and the location shooting. Kate took him aside for a few minutes, kissed him on the cheek and helped him board the plane. When they arrived at Berlin Airport a car was waiting to take them to their hotel. A few blocks away from the Hilton Kate ordered the driver to stop. She got out, walked the rest of the way, entered the hotel by the service entrance and went up to her suite – a common ruse to prevent photographers from snapping her in Spencer's company. She then joined him in Nuremberg.

Soon after their return to America they were approached by producer Ely Landau to play James and Mary Tyrone in a low-budget film version of Eugene O'Neill's mammoth autobiographical play, *Long Day's Journey into Night*, to be directed by Sidney Lumet. Tracy said he would only consider playing it for $500,000, which he knew to be an impossible demand. Perhaps it was his way of turning down a role he would have found too mentally and physically exhausting. (Ralph Richardson was cast instead.) Kate readily accepted $25,000 for about the best role she had been offered for many years.

She had to give a lot of herself, and by the end of the thirty-seven days' shoot, it was she who was physically and mentally exhausted. She made no objection to being photographed unbecomingly, without filters, artful lighting or flattering camera angles. Yet Lumet in his memoirs, *Making Movies*, tells how Kate refused to go to the rushes. ' "Sidney," she said. "I can see how you work... You're...dead honest. You can't protect me. If I go to the rushes all that I'll see is this' – and she reached under her chin and pinched the slightly sagging flesh – "and this" – she did the same thing

Kate as nature intended during rehearsals for Long Day's Journey into Night.

under her arm – "And I need all my strength and concentration to just play the part." '

Kate, brilliantly in command of the role of the tragic mother, later revealed to be a drug addict, never shies away from the ugly realities of the character. The four principals (Hepburn, Richardson, Jason Robards, Dean Stockwell) were awarded a joint best acting award at Cannes, and Kate gained a ninth Oscar nomination.

A short while after the intense shooting of the film, Dr Hepburn died with all his children at his bedside. Kate wrote to Leland Hayward, 'Dad had a stink of a time for nine months. He said, "Thank God it was me and not your mother." He heaved a sigh and was gone with a little sigh... How lucky I have been to have been handed such a remarkable pair in the great shuffle.'

Her mother's death had been more difficult to cope with than her father's. Dr Hepburn's remarriage to Madelaine Santa Croce, the nurse who had worked with him for many years, within months of her mother's death, was seen by Kate as a kind of betrayal of Mrs Hepburn. The great reverence she had felt for him had transferred itself to Tracy.

When Ely Landau went to breakfast with the couple, he found it 'extraordinary to watch her with Spence. She was a totally different person. She turned really submissive – it's the only word I can use – and hardly opened her mouth, other than introducing us.' Once, when they had guests, Kate picked up a log and threw it on the fire. Tracy reprimanded her sharply in front of everybody. She had intruded upon his territory. The guests were astonished to see she was not shamed but sat down beside him more loving than ever. He would call her names like 'bag of bones' or 'Olive Oyl', and ask her to 'shut up for once', and she would accept it from him alone.

In January 1962, *Look* magazine revealed that Tracy was an alcoholic, that he had been living separately from his wife for years and that he and

Kate were 'something more than frequent co-stars'. The article made no impact on the way they lived. They still maintained two homes as a matter of principle, always stayed in separate hotel suites when travelling, and were almost never seen dining out together. They led a quiet life, entertaining only a few intimate friends. Tracy's physical condition improved noticeably, thanks to his abstention from cigarettes and alcohol.

The last hurrah. The final teaming of Tracy and Hepburn, in Stanley Kramer's Guess Who's Coming to Dinner? *(1967).*

But, in July 1963, something happened to make Kate retire from acting for five years. One afternoon, she and Spencer were on their way to a picnic when he suffered a heart attack. She gave him mouth-to-mouth resuscitation until the ambulance arrived. She remembered that on the way to the hospital, Spencer suddenly smiled and said, 'Kate. Isn't this a hell of a way to go to a picnic?' Once he was installed at St Vincent's, she called Mrs Tracy. It was then that each took turns to keep vigil by his bedside. Gradually, Tracy recovered and on his release from hospital Louise left him in Kate's care.

For the next few years, the couple were able to enjoy each other's company without the interruption of work. Although Kate was offered roles which would have satisfied her artistically, she opted to remain beside the man she loved, helping to extend

his life as long as possible and be with him at the end. On days when he visited Louise or she had errands to run, Kate would pack his lunch or dinner in a basket and leave it on his front doorstep. She was also to see that her fridge had a plentiful supply of milk, which Tracy drank, and the daily amount of beer the doctor permitted him. She made him exercise by going for bike rides, or flying kites on windy days.

In September 1965 Tracy was hospitalized again, this time with an inflamed prostate gland requiring surgery. Once again Louise and Kate took it in turns to be with him. All reports of his health were issued to the press by Mrs Tracy. The film colony was prepared for Tracy's imminent death, and spoke in admiring tones of the two women's devotion to him. Miraculously, Tracy improved, so much so that when he had been home for little over a month, Stanley Kramer proposed a script for a film in which Kate and Tracy could co-star again.

The story of *Guess Who's Coming to Dinner?*, about a middle-class WASP couple coming to terms with their daughter's wish to marry a black man, appealed to Kate's liberal sentiments. Spencer left it to Kate to make the decision, and agreed to work on the picture without having read the script. It was good enough

Kate and Spencer waiting around during the making of Guess Who's Coming to Dinner?

Left: *Kate transforming her usual towelled head-dress into Arab wear on the set of* Guess Who's Coming to Dinner?

Right: *With her niece Katharine Houghton, her sister Marion's daughter, seen together as mother and daughter in* Guess Who's Coming to Dinner?

Auntie and niece enjoying a bike ride around the movie lot during the making of Guess Who's Coming to Dinner?

A Life *magazine cover feature captures Kate in buoyant mood to relaunch her career with gusto.*

With Katharine Houghton in
Kate's studio in Hollywood,
studying one of her paintings.
The photos suspended are of
one of Kate's nephews.

for him that Kate was enthusiastic, and that the film urged racial tolerance and understanding, a theme that was dear to his heart. Kate also got Kramer to cast Katharine Houghton, her twenty-three-year-old niece (Marion's daughter), as their daughter.

Stanley Kramer knew that he was taking an enormous risk by hiring Tracy. The insurance company refused to cover the star, whose health they knew to be precarious. Therefore, Kramer personally accepted the responsibility for any financial loss engendered and both he and Kate put up their salaries in lieu of the insurance money, should Tracy die during shooting. Employing the ailing actor became an enormous task of courage for everyone connected with the film. Kate was risking losing Spencer, and Kramer was risking his bank balance and his career.

It was typical of Tracy that he was able to marshal his forces and use all his considerable skills and experience to fulfil his contract admirably. When he delivered the last line of the screenplay to Kate, 'If what they feel for each other is even half what we felt, then that is everything,' she was moved to genuine tears.

When the rather soft-centred *Guess Who's Coming to Dinner?* opened in December 1967 it carried an extra resonance. The critic of the *New York Morning Telegraph* wrote, 'Both of them are splendid, both of them are so beautifully matched... that a lump rises in the throat on the realization that they will never appear together again,' and the *New Yorker* observed that 'when, at its climax, he turns to her and tells her what an old man remembers having loved, it is, for us who are permitted to overhear him, an experience that transcends the theatrical'.

Guess Who's Coming to Dinner? proved to be one of Kate's greatest successes. It grossed many millions of dollars and helped Columbia, which was in

financial difficulties. In the weeks following the conclusion of the shooting, Kate made it a practice to sleep in a small room at the end of a corridor from Spencer's bedroom. She would often leave a light on so that she could get up quickly if he needed anything.

At around 6 a.m. on Saturday 10 June 1967, Tracy had a massive heart attack and died while drinking milk in the kitchen of his home. Kate found him a short time later hunched over the kitchen table. She telephoned the doctor, their friend George Cukor and Tracy's brother Carroll, who in turn contacted Louise. Tracy was moved to the bedroom, where Kate sat alone with him. Ten minutes later, she emerged, her eyes moist with tears, and walked out of the house.

She was not among the congregation that crowded into the Immaculate Heart of Mary Roman Catholic Church to hear the requiem mass held for Tracy, nor among the hundreds of people at the burial at Forest Lawn Cemetery. While Louise stood at the graveside, veiled and in black, Kate remained at home in seclusion. She had debated whether or not to go, but decided that her presence might provoke a field day for reporters and photographers. Forty-eight hours later she went to offer her condolences to Louise and flew back to her family's summer home on the east coast for peace and consolation.

Both Tracy and Hepburn were nominated for Academy Awards in April 1968. Louise, accompanied by her son and daughter, was present at the Oscar ceremony, hoping she would accept the posthumous award for her husband. Kate was in Nice filming *The Madwoman of Chaillot* when the news came that she had won the Academy Award, making her the first three-times winner of the Best Actress Oscar.

'Did Spencer win, too?' she asked. When told he did not, she replied, 'Well, that's OK. I'm sure mine is for the two of us.'

11

A Lioness in Winter

I'm like the Statue of Liberty to a lot of people. When you've been around so long, people identify their whole lives with you. They identify particularly their moments of hope and confidence. It's rather the style now to romanticize certain of the older actors.

The end of Kate's life with Spencer was also a beginning. Faced with the agony of separation by death, she had to take stock. She still had her beloved brothers and sisters, and her friends. There was speculation that Kate would now retire permanently from the screen, but her Puritan temperament wouldn't allow her to surrender to grief, and she turned to work as an antidote to her pain. She felt ready for another good role, which she soon found in the screen adaptation of James Goldman's sub-Shavian historical play *The Lion in Winter*, in which she would portray Eleanor of Aquitaine, the estranged wife of the English king Henry II in twelfth-century France.

Kate carried off her second successive Oscar-winning performance with aplomb, though she occasionally added dollops of sentimentality to her portrayal of the overbearing queen. Certainly, she was able to empathize with the character of a strong-minded, ageing woman, bemoaning her fading beauty, forced to share her husband with another. The *New York Times* thought her 'triumphant in her creation of a complete and womanly queen... a sophisticate whose shrewdness is matched only by her humour'.

Rehearsals for *The Lion in Winter* took place at the Haymarket Theatre in London in October 1967. So enthusiastic was Kate about the project that on one of the first days she rushed through a heavy iron stage door so fast that she slammed it on her hand and smashed her thumb. Hearing her scream, Anthony Harvey, the director, and Peter O'Toole, her co-star, ran over. She was in agony, but she refused to be taken to hospital and insisted on continuing with the rehearsal. Not only had her thumbnail been crushed, but a deep cut ran all the way down her hand. She was out of pain and well enough when *The Lion in Winter* started shooting in Ireland, before shifting to Wales, and then to

A few months after Tracy's death, Kate plunged into work again on The Lion in Winter.

France. The filming was marked by the good-natured but vigorous sparring between Kate and Peter O'Toole, twenty-four years her junior. Witnesses remarked how Kate reduced O'Toole to a shadow of his normally rebellious self. 'She is terrifying,' he remarked. 'It is sheer masochism working with her. She has been sent by some dark fate to nag and torment me.'

Kate dismissed this. 'Don't be silly,' she told him. 'We are going to get on very well. You are Irish and make me laugh. In any case I am on to you and you to me.'

While on location, Kate was indefatigable, constantly showering, swimming, cycling and painting. She had the same routine in the South of France where she had rented a villa in St Jean-Cap Ferrat while making *The Madwoman of Chaillot*. Wearing Spencer Tracy's old

Rehearsing A Lion in Winter *in October 1967 at the Haymarket Theatre in London.*

Right: *On location in France, preparing to bundle up against the medieval cold while shooting* A Lion in Winter.

Opposite: *In the South of France during the making of* The Madwoman of Chaillot *(1969). Nice settings, pity about the film.*

Kate winning her third Best Actress Oscar in the role of the formidable Eleanor of Aquitaine in A Lion in Winter.

All dolled up on the banks of
the Seine for the title role of
The Madwoman of
Chaillot.

sweater, she pedalled about in her slacks and tennis
shoes, going to bed every night at 8.30. To Kate's
disappointment John Huston had walked off the film
just before it went into production, and Bryan Forbes
had been signed only eighteen days before shooting
began.

Supported by a cast that included Charles Boyer,
Paul Henreid, Yul Brynner and Danny Kaye, Kate
softened and sentimentalized the central role of the
madwoman living in the past, going against the grain
of the more caustic character of Jean Giraudoux's
play. Tennessee Williams commented, 'Kate
Hepburn was just not quite old enough or mad
enough to suggest the charisma of lunacy.'

In 1968, Kate announced that she would soon
direct a film called *Martha*, an adaptation of two
related Margery Sharpe novels, about the career of a
gifted girl who goes to France to become a painter.
'This isn't a fantasy,' she told a reporter on the *New
York Times*. 'The fact is that I've always been
interested in directing. Louis B. Mayer quite seriously
asked me to direct films twenty years ago, as did John
Ford, but I've never had a real opportunity to do so
before this.' But although she worked hard to have a
script written and get the film off the ground, it
never came to fruition.

Her next major venture was a return to Broadway
in a musical. Alan Jay Lerner called Garson Kanin to
ask if he could persuade Kate to play the role of the
world-renowned Parisian couturier Coco Chanel.
She was both horrified and intrigued, claiming that
she had never even seen a Broadway musical. But
the challenge was too good a one to pass up.

In preparation, she went to meet Chanel, then in
her mid-eighties, in Paris. 'I was scared to death to
meet her. I had worn the
same clothes for forty
years, literally, even the
shoes. I thought, "If I
don't like her, it will be
agony." ' She need not

*With co-stars Yul Brynner
(standing) and Danny Kaye
on location at Chez Francis
in Paris for* The
Madwoman of Chaillot.

*Kate in a typical black
Chanel dress, posing for Cecil
Beaton's camera in Paris in
1969 in preparation for her
role in the musical* Coco.

As 'the mobled queen' Hecuba
in Euripides' tragedy The
Trojan Women, *shot in
Spain in 1970.*

have worried, and they took to each other immediately, although Coco commented in private to Lerner, 'She's too old for the role. Why, she must be close to sixty!'

On Chanel, Kate remarked, 'She got to me. The essence of her style was simplicity. Exactly what I appreciate most.' Ironically, *Coco* was one of the most expensive shows in Broadway history, far from this essence of simplicity. Although most reviewers attacked the show, Kate's forceful personality, which overcame the limitations of her minimal dancing and her squawking singing voice, won plaudits and packed the theatre for seven months. When the far more suitable Danielle Darrieux took over, audience attendance diminished.

After the Broadway run, Kate made the cast album. When she got home with the disc, she realized she couldn't play it as she didn't own a record player. She called co-star George Rose and said, 'I can't find a Victrolla! Father never believed in them, you know!' Despite her knowledge of contemporary events, and her professional and

Bewigged and in full song in the title role of Coco *at the Mark Hellinger Theatre in 1969, Kate's one and only musical.*

Hecuba, Queen of Troy, in The Trojan Women *(1971), directed by Michael Cacoyannis, in which Kate outranked a distinguished cast of women.*

private contact with much younger people, Kate often seemed to be stuck in the era of her childhood.

In 1970, Kate left for Spain to co-star with Vanessa Redgrave, Irene Papas and Genevieve Bujold in *The Trojan Women* for Greek director Michael Cacoyannis. Asked why she took on the role of Hecuba, the old queen of Troy, she replied, 'My time is running out. And one wants to do everything.' Wearing a torn, dusty, black widow's dress throughout, Kate played up the arrogance of the queen over the more melancholy side. She rarely touched the tragic heights, though when she hisses, 'Kill her!' to decide the fate of Helen of Troy, Kate reveals the power of which she was capable.

Back in the USA, she opened a tour of *Coco* in her home town of Hartford. Returning after an evening performance, Kate, her father's widow and others noticed that a ground-floor window that had previously been closed was open. They went stealthily into the dark house. When Kate reached an upstairs bedroom, a woman jumped out of the closet wielding a hammer. They struggled, and the intruder bit off the end of the index finger of Kate's left hand. The woman made her escape, but Kate recognized her as Luella West, whom she had earlier sacked as a chauffeur. A doctor was called, and the finger, hanging by a thread, was grafted back on.

Kate spent much of her time during the tour planning to appear in a film version of Graham Greene's *Travels with My Aunt*, thrilled at the prospect of working with George Cukor again. But she was fired before shooting began, when the producer felt the role needed a younger woman and cast Maggie Smith instead. Kate thought of suing because 'I don't feel things like that should be allowed to happen. But I thought it was a bore, trying to prove that you've been

misused. One thing that really offended me was to write me a letter to "Katherine". I thought the least he could do when he fired me was to spell my name right.'

In 1971, Garson Kanin's *Tracy and Hepburn – An Intimate Memoir* was published. It was full of personally observed anecdotes that revealed much about the romantic friendship. Kate reeled from the blow. To her, its publication marked a public betrayal by Kanin, placing, as she said, 'a great strain on our friendship'.

Her friendship with John Ford, however, continued as strongly as ever. They had kept in touch over the years, and Ford had even come to New York to see her in *Coco*. In March 1973, as soon as Kate heard Ford had terminal cancer, she went down to see him in Palm Desert, a vacation and retirement community 140 miles from LA, where he had been living a reclusive life for years. He had been married for more than forty-five years to Mary, who had accepted his infidelities just as long as he kept his affairs from becoming public

Tony Richardson (right) directs Kate, Joseph Cotten and Betsy Blair in the TV production of Edward Albee's A Delicate Balance *(1974).*

knowledge. However, she knew his real vice had always been alcohol, not women.

Shocked by Ford's skeletal appearance, and deeply affected by his courage and remaining acerbic wit, Kate spent a week in Palm Desert, talking to him for hours about the old times. The great director was to die five months after Kate's visit.

Now in her mid-sixties, Kate was beginning to get more offers of work, mostly for TV films. The first of three made in London was Edward Albee's *A Delicate Balance*, a savage play about a Connecticut family which fights against the intrusion of two unwanted people. With great intensity, Kate played Agnes, an extremely unsympathetic suburban matron on the verge of insanity. Later, she was to say she accepted the assignment because she wanted to discover what Albee was trying to say in the play.

The entire film was shot in sequence by director Tony Richardson in a large, empty Victorian house near Crystal Palace. The production team tried to

make it as comfortable as possible, but there was no running water, which prevented Kate from taking her constant cold baths and showers. One day, during a break in filming, Kate walked down the hill, and knocked at the door of a house. A woman answered the door.

'Excuse me,' said Kate. 'We're filming in the house up the road, but there is no running water. I wondered whether I could take a bath in your bathroom.' The astonished woman, who recognized the star, asked whether it was a *Candid Camera* prank. Reassured, she allowed Kate to use her bathroom every day throughout the shoot.

Kate was more at ease in Tennessee Williams' *The Glass Menagerie*, but was miscast as Amanda Wingfield, the faded Southern belle. In the scene when Amanda remembers the South, Kate wore the

Laurence Olivier cracks up on the set of the TV movie Love among the Ruins *(1975), directed by George Cukor (right).*

same wedding dress she had worn for the stage performances of *The Philadelphia Story*.

Not long afterwards, George Cukor sent her a script for *Love among the Ruins*, which he had agreed to make for ABC and for which he hoped she might consent to play opposite Laurence Olivier. Osteoarthritis in Kate's hip had been giving her progressive trouble and she had recently submitted to a hip-replacement operation. But the prospect of working with Cukor for the first time in twenty years, and with Olivier for the first time ever, was too irresistible for her to decline. Six months after the surgery, she returned to London to make the film, which had a twenty-day shooting schedule.

To please Kate, Cukor engaged Spencer's daughter, Susie Tracy, as the unit's stills photographer. Kate, who had made a speedy recovery from hip surgery, stayed in the country near the studio and after a day's work would jump on her bicycle and pedal down the nearest country lane. In the extremely slight, old-fashioned but pleasant romantic comedy, Kate played a world-famous Shakespearian actress and Olivier an English barrister. It might have carried more conviction if the roles had been reversed.

In the autumn of 1974, less than a year after her hip surgery, Kate found herself riding a horse and shooting rapids on location in Oregon for *Rooster Cogburn*, opposite John Wayne, Ford's favourite star. Though they were diametrically opposed politically, a deep affection grew up between Kate and 'Duke'. She knew that he had had a lung removed and was being monitored for any sign of the return of the cancer that had been cut away, but he asked for no pity or privileges. Kate spoke of Wayne as 'Self-made. Hard-working. Independent. Of the style of man who blazed trails across our country... They seem to have no patience and no understanding of the more timid and dependent type of person... They don't need or want protection. They dish it out. They take it. Total personal responsibility.' This description might have

fitted the other men in her life such as Tracy, Ford and Hughes.

Wayne commented of his co-star, 'She wants to do everything, too much really, because she can't ride worth a damn and I gotta keep reining in so she can keep up. How she must have been at age twenty-five or thirty! How lucky a man would have been to find her then!'

Rooster Cogburn, in which Kate played a Bible-thumping spinster who learns to use a rifle against marauding bandits to aid a demoted marshal (Wayne), turned out to be a weak retread of *The African Queen*. It was only watchable for the two elderly stars, giving rather self-indulgent performances.

Not long after *Rooster Cogburn*, Kate, as energetic as ever, agreed to appear on Broadway in Enid Bagnold's *A Matter of Gravity* for twelve weeks, as well as touring for a few months before and after the New York engagement. The play was about a wealthy and eccentric woman in her late seventies, with a grandson, a socialist sympathizer, to whom she wishes to leave her estate. A young Christopher Reeve, in his first Broadway play, was cast as the grandson. The future Superman said that Kate greatly influenced him. 'What I learned from her was simplicity. She's a living example that stardom doesn't have to be synonymous with affectation or ego.'

When the play opened in Philadelphia, she and Luddy, who had moved back to his family home a few years earlier, held a reunion after the show. The following morning Luddy met her at her hotel and they had breakfast in her suite. Her ex-husband, now seventy-seven, was ill and ageing, but he was still smartly dressed, and his devotion to Kate had never wavered.

That summer, Kate went to California to make *Olly Olly Oxen Free*, because 'I've always wanted to fly a balloon.' It was charming enough kiddie fare about an

On location in Oregon in **Rooster Cogburn** *(1975) with John Wayne, with whom Kate had a happy time competing.*

Kate as Bible-toting spinster
Eula Goodnight in Rooster
Cogburn.

In Love among the Ruins,
filmed in London for ABC
TV.

Seventy-five-year-old George
Cukor directing sixty-five-
year-old Kate and sixty-
seven-year-old Laurence
Olivier in Love among the
Ruins.

Still wearing the military student's cap which she had picked up on a trip to Europe with Luddy four decades earlier.

eccentric (an adjective continually used for her later roles) old junkyard proprietress who befriends two adventurous youngsters and helps them repair a hot-air balloon, which accidentally takes the three of them aloft for the trip of a lifetime. At the picture's finale, Kate and the two boys descend in the balloon on the Hollywood Bowl concert stage during a rendition of the *1812 Overture*. After the scene was shot, Kate climbed out of the balloon and addressed the audience that filled the Bowl: 'This should prove to all of you that if you're silly enough you can do anything.'

Late in the summer of 1977, Kate went on a visit to London on the invitation of Enid Bagnold, with whom she had struck up a friendship. Bagnold, eighty-six at the time, told Kate frankly that she should have a facelift. After much persuading, Kate travelled incognito up to Scotland to a Glasgow plastic surgeon, who raised the skin beneath her eyes and gave her a slight tuck.

In January 1978, George Cukor came to visit Kate to see if she would work with him once more on another TV production. Cukor, now almost eighty, did not feel he could stand the pressures of a major film. Kate found it difficult to deny Cukor anything, and he suggested they collaborate on Emlyn Williams' *The Corn Is Green*, the inspiring story of an unmarried schoolteacher who helps a young miner gain a scholarship to Oxford. She agreed immediately and pressed to have it filmed in its proper locale – Wales. All the exteriors were shot in Ysbyty Ifan, a small, bleak Welsh village, near the town of Wrexham. Typically, Kate insisted on going down a mine with some of the film crew. They descended 1300 feet in the pitch dark in an open-cage elevator, each carrying a lamp, a gas detector and a gas mask. She talked to the men for a few minutes and then started back up. As they rose in the elevator, 'We heard a beautiful tenor voice start a song. Then

others gradually joined in... It was, in a curious way, both moving and eerie.'

One scene in the film called for Kate to ride a heavy 1890 bicycle up to the top of a steep hill. 'I was humiliated. Nearly had a stroke. But I just could not pump up that hill. Infuriating failure. I have always been able to do my own stuff. But my legs just could not push hard enough to keep that bike from a drunken wobble.' As a result, a twenty-four-year-old woman doubled for Kate. 'They thought that I was silly to be so mad that she could and I couldn't. Yes, I suppose so. But there it is. I still am mad. Damned old legs!'

Although Kate imbued her portrayal of Miss Moffat with idealism and passion, she in no way effaced the memory of Bette Davis's performance in the same role in the 1945 film. Davis had been thirty-seven years old at the time, while Kate, at seventy-two, was too old for the part, and the shaking of her head, due to incipient palsy, was becoming noticeable.

A little later, Cukor sold his house and Tracy's old bungalow. He begged Kate to buy it, but she could not see herself making any more films in California. With John Wayne's death in 1979, there were few of the great old stars left. Two of the survivors were Kate and Henry Fonda. Not only had Kate never acted with Fonda, they had never even met. *On Golden Pond* was to bring them together at last. At their first meeting, Kate walked straight over to Fonda, held out her hand and said, 'Well, it's about time.'

The director, Mark Rydell, and the producers were concerned about Kate's health as well as about Fonda's. Her palsy had progressed, and her head shook involuntarily at more frequent intervals. They finally decided that Kate's palsy would give the elderly wife authenticity, and the starting date was set for June 1980.

Two months before, Kate dislocated her shoulder while playing tennis. The doctors claimed she would

Henry Fonda wearing Spencer Tracy's old hat in On Golden Pond *(1981), Fonda's last film, in which the two old-timers played a bickering but devoted couple.*

Kate protecting herself from the New Hampshire sun on location for On Golden Pond.

As Ethel Thayer in On Golden Pond, *Kate won a record-breaking fourth Best Actress Oscar.*

need a full three months to convalesce and even then a film would be out of the question. 'I knew the film was dependent on the Fonda part being lazy and not working and not wanting to do a lot of physical things. The wife, my part, had to carry all the luggage, do everything, and here I am with an arm that's really bad. Well, I tried to get out of the picture, but Fonda said, "No, you'll be fine. You'll do it. We won't get anyone else." '

With Dorothy Loudon in Ernest Thompson's play West Side Waltz *at the Ethel Barrymore Theatre, New York, in November 1981.*

Amazingly, only two weeks later than planned, filming began on location in New Hampshire. Kate's shoulder healed during the filming, although some days she was in such pain that they had to shoot around her. On the first day, Kate came up to Fonda and said, 'I want you to have this. This was Spencer's favourite hat.' He was moved to tears and wore it throughout the film.

On Golden Pond turned out to be a gentle movie, loved by gerontophiles, anglers and those who cherished the memory of Fonda and Hepburn in films of Hollywood's past. It was also a persuasive look at the fear of approaching death. Fonda, seldom so moving as when he shows his terror of losing his faculties, was exceptional in his last screen role, and Kate, the spiritual centre of the story, was marvellous, too, doddery but placid, full of wisdom, and the quiet strength in the family, although she does seem to be on the verge of tears most of the time and her head shaking is quite noticeable.

Soon after, Kate agreed to return to the stage in *West Side Waltz* by Ernest Thompson, the author of *On Golden Pond*, which dealt with the same theme of ageing. Kate portrayed a widowed former concert pianist living alone in an apartment on the West Side of Manhattan, until a somewhat vulgar middle-aged violinist (Dorothy Loudon) becomes her flat-mate. Playing the piano was marvellous therapy for her shoulder, but at the same time it was difficult, uncomfortable and frustrating. She and Loudon rehearsed daily at Kate's house, practising the piano and violin together as well. Determinedly, Kate practised three to four hours a day, regaining the mobility of her fingers, memorizing the intricacies of each piece, striving to achieve the appearance of a professional pianist at work.

The conventional Broadway play opened in New York on 8 November 1981 for a limited three-month engagement, and received lukewarm reviews. Again, despite the material, Kate gained praise. Walter Kerr in the *New York Times* wrote, 'One mysterious thing she has learned to do is breathe unchallengeable life into lifeless lines. She does it, or seems to do it, by giving the most serious consideration to every syllable she utters. There may have been a time when she coasted on mannerisms, turned on her rhythms into a form of rapid transit. That time is long gone.'

A little over a year later Kate suffered another accident. Driving on slippery icy roads in Fenwick, she hit a pole. The impact crumpled the front end of the car and a piece of steel nearly severed her right foot. When help came and Kate was extricated from the car and transferred to an ambulance, her foot 'was hanging just from a tendon'.

She insisted she be taken to Hartford Hospital, an hour's ride over icy roads, where the surgeon who had saved her finger was on the staff. He was alerted and immediately performed intricate surgery to reattach the foot. The foot was saved, but for the next eight months she spent equal time in and out of hospital. After six more months of therapy (and the news that Luddy had just died), she decided to go back to work.

Kate had long wanted to do *The Ultimate Solution of Grace Quigley*, a black comedy about an elderly woman who hires a hit man (Nick Nolte) to help her put an end to the lives of her ageing companions, who no longer care to live. The script, by Martin Zweiback, had been literally dumped on her back doorstep when she had occupied the California bungalow eleven years earlier. She had tried to get it produced, but euthanasia was considered too controversial a subject.

The film finally started shooting in October 1983. Nolte called Kate 'a cranky old broad, but a lot of fun'. She had to tackle without a double a scene that called for her to ride a motorcycle with Nolte, but she did it, as well as braving harsh conditions of shooting on location in New York during a particularly cold autumn.

Unfortunately, the film fails to come off, either as a plea for mercy killing or as a black comedy, being neither pointed nor funny enough. But Kate's glowing eyes, wobbly head and shaky voice bring an element of otherworldliness to the role. On the theme of the film, Kate commented that she personally had no fear of death. 'What release! To sleep is the greatest joy there is... If I were a burden to myself and I could leave my money to younger people who could really use it, I would feel it was my privilege to do what I could do... If my own mother had been desperately ill and attached to a lot of humiliating machines, I think I would have shot her.'

However, despite the themes of her last two films, Kate, a comparatively healthy seventy-seven-year-old, was not ready to contemplate death, or even retirement, just yet.

Always ready to try something new, seventy-seven-year-old Kate clings to Nick Nolte in The Ultimate Solution of Grace Quigley *(1984).*

Left: *In the title role of* The Ultimate Solution of Grace Quigley, *a black comedy on the theme of euthanasia, a subject close to Kate's heart.*

Right: *Still holding the screen in one of her last TV movies,* The Man Upstairs *(1992).*

12

Twilight of a Goddess

Isn't it fun getting older is really a terrible fallacy. That's like saying I prefer driving an old car with a flat tyre.

Few people passing the four-storey Manhattan brownstone house on East 49th Street would suspect that it is the New York home of one of the cinema's greatest stars. This East Side area, known as Turtle Bay – the original bay has long been filled in – may be an elite area now, but it was considerably run down when Katharine Hepburn moved there in the early 1930s.

Huge windows look out on to a back garden of trees and flowers, most of it upkept by Kate herself. Although she has a cook, a chauffeur and a secretary, she prefers to do much of her own cooking, shopping and organizing herself, and to be alone for a good deal of the day. The comfortable yet simply furnished living room, always filled with vases of freshly picked flowers, has two large white sofas, a few antique chairs, Persian rugs and, on the walls, besides a portrait of Ethel Barrymore by John Singer Sargent, hang many oil paintings executed by Kate herself. A vast bald eagle stands on the mantelpiece. None of her four Oscars is anywhere to be seen.

On the dressing table of her third-floor bedroom is a framed photograph of Dr Hepburn; a photograph of Spencer Tracy sits on the bedside table. On the wall is a portrait of Tracy painted by Kate in the Sixties, as well as a small bronze bust she made of him. In the small basement kitchen are more photographs of friends and co-stars of yesteryear.

The composer Stephen Sondheim, a next-door neighbour, shares the communal garden. Some years ago, Kate was woken up in the early hours of the morning by Sondheim, who was busy working at the piano on the score of *Pacific Overtures*. Wrapping a robe around her, Kate went out into the garden and placed her nose against one of Sondheim's windows. The composer and a companion froze when they caught sight of her, standing and staring at them. Kate disappeared as quickly as she had appeared, but she had made her point. From then on,

In serene old age, Kate continued to lead a full life, even acting from time to time.

Sondheim was careful not to play the piano late at night.

Never one to shy away from controversy, Kate spent a great deal of her time working for Planned Parenthood, thus carrying on the work of her mother. 'Things are getting worse,' she proclaimed. 'Now they've even changed the rules about when a foetus is alive – although I've never seen a religious service for a miscarriage, have you?'

As she entered her eighties, Kate began to limit her acting appearances to the odd television role. She was only seen in public on rare occasions. When she did go to the theatre or a movie, she generally made sure few people would recognize her. Ironically, however, there were two well-reported occasions when she drew attention to herself in public.

One evening, she and her director friend Anthony Harvey attended a performance of a minimalist production of Leonard Bernstein's *Candide*. Like the rest of the audience, she was forced to sit on one of the rows of wooden seats. At the intermission, Kate rose from her seat, walked on the stage and reclined on a canopied bed that was part of the set. She had been suffering back pain, and it was her way of protesting at the discomfort of the seating. It added to her reputation of being slightly dotty. However, she told a reporter, 'The young always think their elders are eccentric.'

The other of her very public displays was when she came out of a movie on 58th Street to find her car hemmed in by a double-parked truck. She decided that her only means of escape was to drive her car on to the sidewalk and make a sharp turn. Many of the people waiting to get into the theatre recognized her, and they stood back to make room for her and see what she would do. 'I gave it the gas,' she explained, 'aimed at the crowd and turned amid cheers – "That's it, Katie, ride 'em!" It was thrilling.'

Although Kate would have enjoyed working more, she found the scripts she was offered far too

Happily relaxing in her comfortable New York home on East 49th Street, where she has lived since the 1930s.

Portrait of the most unpretentious of Hollywood legends.

With Anthony Quinn in the semi-autobiographical TV movie This Can't Be Love *(1993), in which she played an Oscar-winning film star in retirement.*

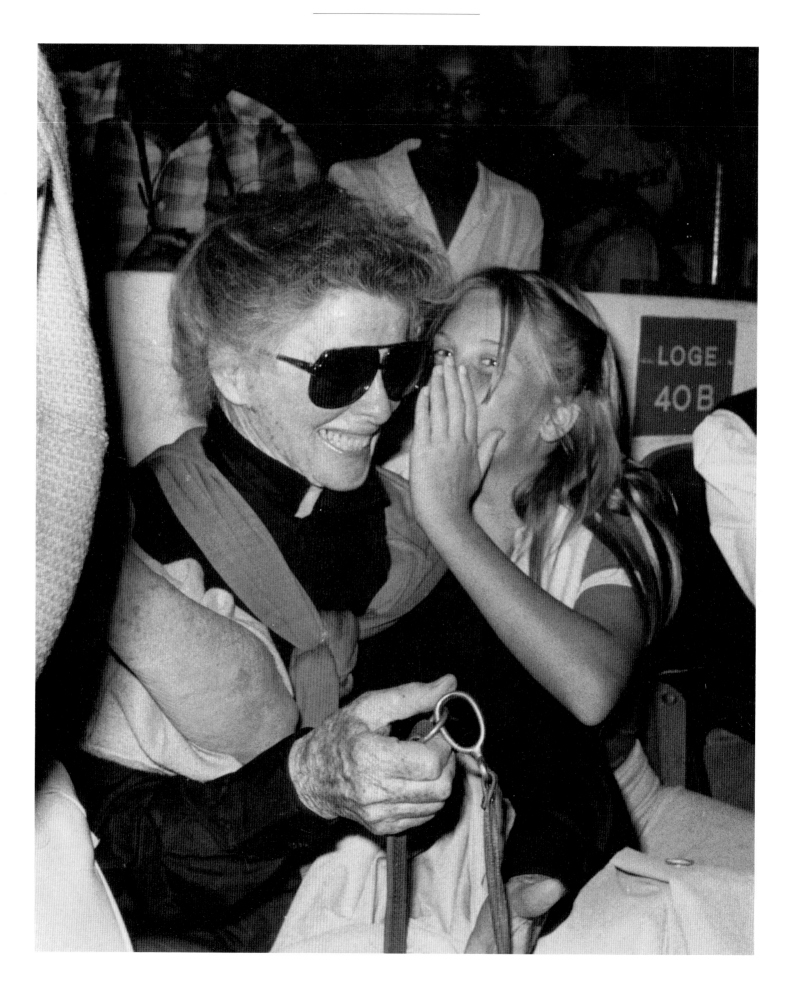

Kate enjoys a secret with
her niece Patricia at
New York's Madison
Square Garden at a concert
by the Jackson Five in
August 1981.

distasteful or exploitative. When many actresses of her age were reduced to playing Grande Guignol murderesses in tawdry horror movies, pathetic old people or bit parts, Kate had continued to play leading roles in prestigious films. Now she refused to appear in anything that offended her professional and personal standards. 'The assumption is that the audience is totally uninspired, and that pornography and depravity are all they want to see. I find it offensive and very sad that producers and actors are so willing to sell out for the money... It's awfully easy in the entertainment field to talk yourself into justifying the degrading things you do.'

She had been uncomfortable with a speech in *A Delicate Balance* in which she had to express her distress at her husband's predilection for coitus interruptus, and the only 'four-letter' word she had uttered in her career had been in *Coco*. As the curtain went up at the beginning of the second act, Kate strode down a staircase, crossed over to the footlights, stared at the audience and exclaimed, 'Shit!' Then she turned on her heel and walked off the stage to gales of laughter and applause. The amused reaction came about merely because the word had been uttered by Katharine Hepburn.

Kate, with false naivety, even seemed to deny the existence of homosexuality. This from someone with advanced views, a close friend

Fighting off photographers
while attending a
performance of 42nd Street
at the Winter Garden
Theatre in October 1980.

of George Cukor, an intimate of Noël Coward, Tennessee Williams and Robert Helpmann, a participant in *Suddenly Last Summer*, and an actress whose gay fans were legion.

One script for a TV movie that appealed to her greatly was *This Can't Be Love*, which was written for her and which verged on the autobiographical. With natural warmth and humour, Kate played an Oscar-winning film star in retirement, who spends many of her days painting. She mourns the death of her elder brother (in World War I), talks about growing up a tomboy, reminisces about working with George Cukor and John Ford, and acting with John Wayne, recalls her affection for George Bernard Shaw, and when she looks in the mirror says, 'No one ever knew what to do with this face.'

When Warren Beatty first called Kate to ask if she would play the cameo role of his Aunt Ginny in the second remake of *Love Affair*, she answered the phone by saying, 'What do *you* want?' in an abrupt manner. She refused the offer, explaining that she had never taken a supporting role or a small one. Undeterred, Beatty showered her with presents and flowers, and flew to New York to see her on a number of occasions. After he had promised to send his private jet to take her from New York to the Warner Bros studio set in California, she finally capitulated. Looking remarkably spry, though her head shook badly, Kate gamely did her bit in a scene when would-be married couple Beatty and Annette Bening pay her a visit on a Pacific island, in order to obtain her blessing. Critics failed to give the redundant and soppy film their blessing, but Kate

escaped unscathed by the experience. It was to be her swan song.

Kate was now happy to spend her days reading, doing the gardening, and visiting her family in Connecticut at weekends. 'We're very limited by this box we came in,' she once said. 'The box is me and it is gradually rotting away... When the vital things go, it dissolves. You'd have to be a fool not to recognize that.' She continued to see death as 'the big sleep', an idea she found not at all frightening.

Katharine Hepburn had been a star for over six decades, and generation after generation of movie-goers has been aware of her. In 1995, in a poll conducted among fifty critics worldwide and the general public by the *Guardian* newspaper, Kate was selected as the greatest woman film star ever, alive or dead. She topped a similar poll among film-makers in *Time Out* magazine a few months later. She achieved this reputation through her innate talent, but also through a tenacious character, possibly formed by her upbringing in an atmosphere of complete spiritual freedom and Spartan physical discipline. She was determined to have her own way in an industry noted for compromise and commercial priorities. Even when at her lowest ebb, she refused to accept defeat, nor was she willing to pander to the media's insatiable appetite for prurient gossip. She had pursued her career on her own honourable, dignified and exacting terms, and it paid off.

'Go out and make life interesting,' Dr Hepburn once told his daughter. By following his advice, Katharine Houghton Hepburn made our lives more interesting as well.

Leaving the Ethel Barrymore
Theatre after a performance
of West Side Waltz *in*
November 1981. Au revoir,
Kate!

(N.B. Dates given are release dates in USA. Names in parentheses are roles played by K.H.)

1932
A Bill of Divorcement (Sydney Fairfield)
Director: George Cukor
(RKO)

1933
Christopher Strong (Lady Cynthia Darrington)
Director: Dorothy Arzner
(RKO)
Morning Glory (Eva Lovelace)
Director: Lowell Sherman
(RKO)
Little Women (Jo March)
Director: George Cukor
(RKO)

1934
Spitfire (Trigger Hicks)
Director: John Cromwell
(RKO)
The Little Minister (Babbie)
Director: Richard Wallace
(RKO)

1935
Break of Hearts (Constance Dane)
Director: Philip Moeller
(RKO)
Alice Adams (Alice Adams)
Director: George Stevens
(RKO)

1936
Sylvia Scarlett (Sylvia Scarlett)
Director: George Cukor
(RKO)
Mary of Scotland (Mary Stuart)
Director: John Ford
(RKO)
A Woman Rebels (Pamela Thistlewaite)
Director: Mark Sandrich
(RKO)

1937
Quality Street (Phoebe Throssel)
Director: George Stevens
(RKO)
Stage Door (Terry Randall)
Director: Gregory La Cava
(RKO)

1938
Bringing Up Baby (Susan Vance)
Director: Howard Hawks
(RKO)
Holiday (Linda Seton)
Director: George Cukor
(Columbia)

1940
The Philadelphia Story (Tracy Lord)
Director: George Cukor
(MGM)

1942
Woman of the Year (Tess Harding)
Director: George Stevens
(MGM)
Keeper of the Flame (Christine Forrest)
Director: George Cukor

1943
Stage Door Canteen (Herself)
Director: Frank Borzage
(United Artists)

1944
Dragon Seed (Jade)
Directors: Jack Conway and Harold S. Bucquet
(MGM)

1945
Without Love (Jamie Rowan)
Director: Harold S. Bucquet
(MGM)

1946
Undercurrent (Ann Hamilton)
Director: Vincente Minnelli
(MGM)

1947
The Sea of Grass (Lutie Cameron)
Director: Elia Kazan
(MGM)
Song of Love (Clara Wieck Schumann)
Director: Clarence Brown
(MGM)

1948
State of the Union (Mary Matthews)
Director: Frank Capra
(MGM)

1949
Adam's Rib (Amanda Bonner)
Director: George Cukor
(MGM)

1951
The African Queen (Rose Sayer)
Director: John Huston
(United Artists)

1952
Pat and Mike (Pat Pemberton)
Director: George Cukor
(MGM)

1955
Summertime (Jane Hudson)
Director: David Lean
(United Artists)

1956
The Rainmaker (Lizzie Curry)
Director: Joseph Anthony
(Paramount)
The Iron Petticoat (Vinka Kovelenko)
Director: Ralph Thomas
(MGM)

1957
The Desk Set (Bunny Watson)
Director: Walter Lang
(Twentieth Century-Fox)

1959
Suddenly Last Summer (Mrs Venable)
Director: Joseph L. Mankiewicz
(Columbia)

1962
Long Day's Journey into Night (Mary Tyrone)
Director: Sidney Lumet
(Embassy)

1967
Guess Who's Coming to Dinner? (Christina Drayton)
Director: Stanley Kramer
(Columbia)

1968
The Lion in Winter (Eleanor of Aquitaine)
Director: Anthony Harvey
(Avco Embassy)

1969
The Madwoman of Chaillot (Aurelia)
Director: Bryan Forbes
(Warner Bros–Seven Arts)

1971
The Trojan Women (Hecuba)
Director: Michael Cacoyannis
(Cinerama Releasing)

1975
Rooster Cogburn (Eula Goodnight)
Director: Stuart Miller
(Universal)

1978
Olly Olly Oxen Free (Miss Pudd)
Director: Richard A. Colla
(Sanrio Film Distribution)

1981
On Golden Pond (Ethel Thayer)
Director: Mark Rydell
(Universal)

1984
The Ultimate Solution of Grace Quigley (Grace Quigley)
Director: Anthony Harvey
(MGM/UA)

1994
Love Affair (Aunt Ginny)
Director: Glen Gordon Caron
(Warner Bros)

THEATRE

1928
The Czarina (Lady-in-Waiting)
by Melchior Lengyel and Lajos Biro
The Cradle Snatchers (Flapper)
by Russell Medcraft and Norma Mitchell
The Big Pond (Barbara. Fired after one performance)
by George Middleton and A. E. Thomas
These Days (Veronica Sims)
by Katharine Clugston
Holiday (understudy to Hope Williams. Played one performance as Linda Seton)
by Philip Barry

1929
Death Takes a Holiday (Grazia)
by Alberto Casella

1930
A Month in the Country (Katia)
by Ivan Turgenev
The Admirable Crichton (Lady Agatha Lasenby)
by J. M. Barrie
The Romantic Young Lady (Amalia)
by Martinez Sierra
Romeo and Juliet (Kinswoman to the Capulets)
by William Shakespeare
Art and Mrs Bottle (Judy Bottle)
by Benn W. Levy

1931
The Animal Kingdom (Daisy Sage)
by Philip Barry

1932
The Warrior's Husband (Antiope)
by Julian Thompson
The Bride the Sun Shines on (Psyche Marbury)
by Will Cotton

1933
The Lake (Stella Surrege)
by Dorothy Massingham and Murray MacDonald

1936
Jane Eyre (Jane Eyre)
by Charlotte Brontë

1939
The Philadelphia Story (Tracy Lord)
by Philip Barry

1942
Without Love (Jamie Coe Rowan)
by Philip Barry

1950
As You Like It (Rosalind)
by William Shakespeare

1952
The Millionairess (Epifania)
by George Bernard Shaw

1957
The Merchant of Venice (Portia)
by William Shakespeare
Much Ado About Nothing (Beatrice)
by William Shakespeare

1960
Twelfth Night (Viola)
by William Shakespeare
Antony and Cleopatra (Cleopatra)
by William Shakespeare

1969
Coco ('Coco' Chanel)
by Alan Jay Lerner (book and lyrics) and André Previn (music)

1976
A Matter of Gravity (Mrs Basil)
by Enid Bagnold

1981
West Side Waltz (Margaret Mary Elderdice)
by Ernest Thompson

TELEVISION

1973
The Glass Menagerie (Amanda Wingfield)
Director: Anthony Harvey
A Delicate Balance (Agnes)
Director: Tony Richardson

1975
Love among the Ruins (Jessica Medlicott)
Director: George Cukor

1979
The Corn Is Green (Miss Moffat)
Director: George Cukor

1986
Mrs Delafield Wants to Marry (Mrs Delafield)
Director: George Schaefer

1992
The Man Upstairs (Victoria)
Director: George Schaefer

1993
This Can't Be Love (Marion Bennett)
Director: Anthony Harvey

ACADEMY AWARDS AND NOMINATIONS
(Winning titles in bold)

1932-33 **Morning Glory**
1935 Alice Adams
1940 The Philadelphia Story
1942 Woman of the Year
1951 The African Queen
1955 Summertime
1956 The Rainmaker
1959 Suddenly Last Summer
1962 Long Day's Journey into Night
1967 **Guess Who's Coming to Dinner?**
1968 **The Lion in Winter**
1981 **On Golden Pond**

INDEX

PICTURE ACKNOWLEDGEMENTS

Archive Photos Stock Photo Library, New York
Associated Press, London
Photograph by Cecil Beaton courtesy of Sotheby's,
       London
Camera Press, London, with acknowledgement to: Cecil
       Beaton, John Bryson
Joel Finler
Burt Glinn/Magnum Photos
Bob Henriques/Magnum Photos
George Hoyningen-Huene
David Hurn/Magnum Photos
The Kobal Collection, London
London Features International
David McGough/LFI
Photofest, New York
Pictorial Press, London
Range/UPI/Bettmann
Rex Features, London, with acknowledgement to: Araldo
       di Crollalanza, Joel Elkings, Globe, Sipa Press,
       Ruan O'Lochlainn, Don Ornitz, Anita Weber
Terence Spencer/*Life* magazine © Time Warner Inc.
Dennis Stock/Magnum Photos

BFI Stills, Posters and Designs, London, with acknowl-
edgement to: ABC/TV, American Film Theater, Avco-
Embassy, Cannon Film Inc., Cinerama Releasing
Corporation, Columbia Pictures, Embassy Pictures,
Metro-Goldwyn-Mayer, MGM/UA/Cannon Films,
Paramount Pictures, PNC TV, RKO Radio Pictures Inc.,
Time Warner Inc., Turner Entertainment Corporation,
Twentieth Century-Fox, United Artists Corporation,
Universal/AFD, Universal Pictures, Warner Brothers,
Warner Brothers-Seven Arts

Every reasonable effort has been made to acknowledge
the ownership of copyrighted photographs included in
this volume. Any errors that have inadvertently occurred
will be corrected in subsequent editions provided notifica-
tion is sent to the publisher.

9/00